HISTORY IN CAMERA

Wedding Fashions 1860-1980

Avril Lansdell

Shire Publications Ltd

Copyright © 1983 by Avril Lansdell. First published 1983. Second edition 1986. ISBN 0 85263 839 6.

Set in 11 on 11 point Times roman and printed in Great Britain by C. I. Thomas & Sons (Haverfordwest) Ltd, Press Buildings, Merlins Bridge, Haverfordwest, Dyfed.

Front cover: *Ethel Dorothy Smith and William Thomas Taylor at Surbiton on Easter Monday, 28th March 1910, photographed in the garden after their wedding. The bridegroom wore a frock coat over dark trousers and waistcoat and carried a top hat. The report of the wedding in the local paper described the bride as wearing 'a Princesse dress of hyacinth blue chiffon merve (a rich satin)'. She carried a sheaf of white lilies. (See also picture 37.)*

Title page: *A debutante bride of 1902, Mrs Muriel Dams, poses for a London studio portrait in a dress that is a froth of delicate silk and lace.*

Below: *An unknown soldier from New Zealand married a girl from Walton-on-Thames, Surrey, when convalescing at the Mount Felix Hospital in Walton in 1916. He and his best man wore their uniforms, while she wore her best dress and a plain hat. She poses with a black kitten on her lap, for luck.*

Opposite: *A 1928 studio group showing the wedding party of Arthur and Bessie Ranger at Strood, Kent. Bride and bridesmaids wore short dresses, the bride's being of white satin with a scalloped hem. Her veil, held well down on her forehead, hung to the hem of her dress, as did the trails of fern on her long bouquet. Her groom, a shipwright at Chatham Dockyard, wore a lounge suit.*

Contents

Detail from 'The Photographer's Studio', a painting of the 1870s showing a newly married couple posing for their wedding photograph. Note the overhead daylight illumination; Victorian photographers' studios were normally at the tops of buildings to gain the advantage of sky lighting.

1. Introduction: wedding photography

Weddings are social occasions that have been celebrated from antiquity with feasting and ritual. Ballad writers and poets have commemorated weddings; music has been composed for them and plays written about them. Newspapers have reported them, painters have recorded them and so, above all, have photographers. From the official royal ceremonial photograph to the humble snapshot or modern colour slide, almost every family in Great Britain, of any faith or none, has wedding photographs tucked away somewhere. Bringing them out evokes many memories and we look at them with tears or laughter.

Many people believe that the conventional white wedding with a bevy of bridesmaids, church service, family ritual and special, different clothes is a tradition handed down from the middle ages, unchanged and unchanging. But the only ancient tradition is that a wedding is a celebration. The white wedding, like many twentieth-century traditions, originated with the Victorians, and, like many nineteenth-century innovations, it was enthusiastically continued and elaborated by the Edwardians.

The earliest known photograph of a bride in her wedding dress was taken by a Boston daguerreotype photographer in 1854. The first known photograph of bridesmaids is that of the young women attending Queen Victoria's eldest daughter, Princess Vicky, at her wedding to the German Crown Prince Frederick in 1858.

Since that unknown bride and the aristocratic young bridesmaids of those early photographs a host of other Victorians have come down to us, recorded by the camera in their own time and saved for our eyes by the Victorian passion for collecting photographs of all their numerous relatives and keeping them in albums. Queen Victoria set the pattern and even the humblest of her subjects attempted to follow her. These family albums were continued by the Edwardians and many of them from all parts of the British Isles provide the photographs in this book. Over the past one hundred and twenty years the styles and settings of the photographs in these albums have changed almost as much as the clothes worn by the subjects. Most Victorian photographs of people were taken in a studio. They cover all social classes, for the studio portraits, especially the small cartes-de-visite, were comparatively cheap. It is often difficult to tell the social class of the sitters for they would have worn their best clothes for the occasion and posed against standard, stereotyped backgrounds.

SAMUEL FRY, & Co.,
PHOTOGRAPHIC ART STUDIO,
9, *SURBITON PARK TERRACE*,
SURBITON.

PORTRAITS DAILY FROM 10 TILL DUSK.

THE Public are invited to inspect a PERMANENT PUBLIC EXHIBITION of WORKS of ART in PHOTOGRAPHY produced by S. Fry and Co., at the above address, including Portraits of all sizes, and highly-finished Porcelain and Carbon Pictures ; also Landscapes and Views of Houses, for which appointments can be made.

Enlarged Pictures are made on the premises daily, and a great variety can be seen in Oils, Crayon, and Water Colour. Wedding Parties photographed at any distance. Copies of old or faded pictures made and enlarged.

---

1. *A photographer's advertisement from the 'Surrey Comet' of 8th May 1875.*

Group photographs taken out of doors gained in popularity as the cumbersome equipment of the early daguerreotype photographer gave way to the more portable apparatus of the wet collodion process. Although the equipment was portable, the outdoor photographer of the 1860s and 1870s had nonetheless to take a complete darkroom with him, for the glass plates used in this process had first to be coated with collodion containing potassium iodide and then sensitised by being dipped into a bath of silver nitrate solution. This plate had then to be exposed while still moist as the sensitivity was lost as the collodion dried. The photographer's darkroom often consisted of a small handcart covered with a black tent into which he put the upper part of his body so that he could work in the dark, in a garden or any landscape setting, producing negatives on the spot. The prints were made back at his studio, at a later date.

In spite of these difficulties commercial photographers did take pictures out of doors; these included wedding groups, in gardens, from the late 1860s onwards and the photographers proudly advertised the fact. However most Victorian wedding photographs taken in garden settings depict wealthy families, as can be seen from the types of houses and gardens revealed in the photographs.

As photography became more popular and cheaper the outdoor wedding group became more common. Edwardian albums show a wide range of weddings, from wealthy people taken in beautiful gardens, as in the 1860s and 1870s, to street groups in London, seated on hard chairs outside the local shops, or northern families ranged on the front steps, with bride and bridegroom on chairs in the centre and everyone else in rows above them, almost always with someone peering through the curtains.

Photographs showing bride and groom leaving the church first appeared in the 1920s and these grew more popular until by the 1960s photographs were being taken inside the church as well. Registry offices have been used for weddings since the reign of William IV, but such weddings were comparatively rare until the twentieth century and have only become common since the Second World War. Photographs taken inside registry offices also seem to date from the 1960s onwards.

Since the Second World War, as the class system has died away, people have wanted to record the occupational or interest groups to which they belong and so 'recognition' wedding ceremonial has grown up, notably that of friends of the bride or groom forming a guard of honour outside the church or registry office door so that the newly married couple walk under an archway of objects associated with them. This is a popular subject for wedding photographs and from the 1940s onwards brides and grooms are shown under archways of such objects as tin hats, truncheons, swords, rowing blades and tennis rackets. So popular has this kind of ceremony become that the Ministry of Defence has issued a pamphlet giving instructions on the correct way of forming an archway of swords at a wedding.

Published newspaper accounts of society weddings date back for more than two hundred years, and for more ordinary people about one hundred years. The Dougall scrapbooks, a collection of newspaper cuttings and photographs of all kinds compiled by Mrs George Harvey Jay (formerly a Miss Brownrigg) and continued by her daughter Mrs Walter Dougall, record the events

2 (above left). *In the early years of the twentieth century Harold Ellis married Sarah Lovesey at Nottingham (left). He wore black trousers and frock coat over a striped roll-collared waistcoat and carried a top hat and gloves. Sarah wore a white dress with a softly bloused top, a high neck and three-quarter length frilled sleeves. Her skirt, decorated with three frills, was gathered at the sides and back to a shaped and fitted waistband. Her veil was laid over piled-up hair and she carried a trailing 'shower' bouquet.*

3 (above right). *Their son, Donald, born after the First World War, was married at the end of the 1939-45 war to Dorothy Hobbs at St Mark's church, Dalston, London. The date was 25th August 1945 and he was still in uniform. His bride wore a plain long white dress with a 'sweetheart' neckline that revealed a two-strand pearl necklace. Her long sleeves were gathered into cuffs at the wrist, while her veil was held well back on short curled hair with a pearl and flower tiara. Her bouquet was a spray, cradled in her hands with one long trail of fern. The bridesmaids (there were two) had similar dresses but with short sleeves.*

4 (opposite). *A studio photograph of a 1925 bride. This very fashionable dress is now in Carlisle Museum and is of peach silk crepe, hand embroidered with white glass beads and ivory silk thread. It had a wide boat-shaped neckline with a turned-down collar. The sleeves, unseen in this photograph, are short. The waistline is low, with a tie belt at the hips, also unseen in the picture. The length is mid-calf and the dress was pulled on over the head with no fastenings. The veil and shoes were pale pink but have not survived. The bouquet was of white lilies and pink gladioli.*

5 (above). *Marjorie Blakeley married Louis Cyril Blakey at Church Fenton Methodist chapel, North Yorkshire, on 25th September 1933. The bridegroom wore grey trousers and a black coat (probably morning dress) with a pale grey tie and a wing collar. The bride had a white lace dress and a long veil. The two older bridesmaids wore long 'garden party' dresses with double cape short sleeves and picture hats, while the two younger bridesmaids wore long dresses with skirts composed of rows of little frills. Their short sleeves are plain and they wear wreaths of rosebuds in their hair. The guests are in typical early 1930s clothes. Note the length of the women's skirts and the fox fur round the shoulders of the guest on the right of the group posing outside the church.*

6 (right). *Dorothy Daniell and Stanley Hanning were married in Plymouth in 1933. He was the captain of the crew of a gentleman's yacht and wore clothes in the style of a naval uniform (button three, show four), with brass insignia buttons probably to a design of his house or yacht squadron. Dorothy was a housekeeper and wore a mid-calf length dress in a lace design, with a small pull-on hat. Their photograph was taken in a photographer's studio.*

7. *Third Officer Cynthia Discombe of the WRNS married Surgeon Lieutenant Courtney Remington-Hobbs of the RNVR on 3rd March 1942. They are pictured in full uniform leaving the naval establishment's tin chapel beneath a guard of honour of fellow officers all holding dress swords to form an archway. This was an official War Office released photograph intended to raise public morale by showing that love and fellowship continued even in the midst of war.*

and occasions of the Brownrigg, Jay and Dougall families during the period 1873 to 1942. They were well connected military and society people whose sporting activities were published in *The Field,* whose military promotions were reported in *The Times,* with births, deaths and marriage announcements, and whose weddings were described in *The Queen* and *The Ladies' Pictorial* as well as *The Times* and other newspapers.

Although the published descriptions of these weddings are very precise and include lists of guests and wedding presents as well as details of the clothes worn by brides, their mothers and the bridesmaids, the earliest published photograph of a bride in her wedding dress in the Dougall scrapbooks was in 1894 (picture 26). Before that, and for some time after, the accounts of society weddings were illustrated with head and shoulders portraits of the bride and groom in day or evening dress, although ladies' magazines would have full-page sketches of wedding clothes.

8 (left). *Miss Muriel Dorothea Forbes, posing for a studio portrait in the dress in which she was married to Henry Vaughan Anthony at Limpsfield parish church in 1906. Her dress was of soft ivory silk voile made up of many frills mounted on an underdress of a stiffer ivory taffeta. The skirt was of the same fabrics, the narrow frills starting at knee level. It is possible that she wore this dress as an evening dress after her wedding, for it is unusual that an Edwardian wedding dress should have had a low neck and elbow sleeves. For her wedding she may well have worn a high-necked, long-sleeved chemisette under this bodice.*

9 (right). *Mrs Anthony's grand-daughter Harriet was married in 1956 in a lace dress mounted on a foundation made from the underskirt of the dress in picture 8. Harriet's dress was cut with the mid 1950s fashionable low waistline to the fitted, high-necked bodice, which had a row of small satin-covered buttons on the back of the bodice and the inside of the sleeves. She wore a circlet of orange blossom on her head, with a waist-length veil fastened to the back of it so that it did not cover the top of her head. Both Harriet's dress and the bodice of her grandmother's dress are in Weybridge Museum.*

Newspapers carried photographic supplements from the turn of the century and royal weddings were featured in these, but the daily papers (other than the *Daily Mirror*) and local weekly newspapers had few photographs of any kind until the 1940s. During the Second World War the Ministry of Information periodically released photographs 'taken somewhere in England' of the weddings of notable service personnel, together with a suitable text designed to boost public morale.

Since the end of the Second World War in 1945, however, almost every local newspaper in the British Isles has, every week, shown photographs of local brides and grooms in their wedding clothes. Everybody loves a wedding, whether their own or somebody else's, and this book is a record of the wedding fashions of the one hundred and twenty years from 1860 to 1980.

2. The Victorian wedding, 1860-1900

Sweetly simple, 1860-70

Queen Victoria kept careful records of her family. Their deeds, thoughts and appearance have come down to us in her journals, her drawings and the many photographs she commissioned. There are no photographs of her own wedding. The first royal photographs are two daguerreotypes of Prince Albert made in 1842, and the first photograph of the Queen was taken in 1844. But the weddings of all the royal children were photographed and their clothes set the fashion for all the other Victorian brides who could afford to copy royalty. The eldest daughter, Princess Vicky, was married in a grand ceremony in 1858, but the wedding of her younger sister, Princess Alice, to Prince Louis of Hesse in 1862 was a much more sombre occasion, for the Prince Consort had died unexpectedly in 1861 and the marriage took place during the period of mourning. The match had been arranged before Prince Albert's death and he himself had designed a veil for his daughter, who wore it, thrown back from her face, above a simple crinoline dress of white lace. The Queen, however, wore deep mourning and the women guests wore grey or violet dresses, while the gentlemen, including the bridegroom, wore black tailcoats and neckcloths, grey trousers and white waistcoats. The bride changed back into mourning after the ceremony, although she was photographed in her wedding dress for the royal family album first.

Most 1860s weddings were more colourful. In 1861 Ministers' *Gazette of Fashion* had decreed that bridegrooms or gentlemen attending weddings should wear 'frock coats of blue, claret or mulberry colour, with or without a velvet collar, single-breasted waistcoats of white quilling, plain, corded or with a pattern, or white drill. Trousers of pale drab or lavender doeskin.' The magazine went on to lament that 'unfortunately invisible green or even *black* coats are occasionally seen at weddings but both are inconsistent with the occasion except in the case of the marriage of a clergyman', or, of course, during a period of mourning. Although many brides wore white, following royal precedence, colour was to predominate in fashionable men's wedding clothes, with the trousers in a lighter colour than the coat, well into the 1890s. The top hat was the normal headwear for weddings, but it could be blue, black, white or grey as the wearer fancied.

The fashion magazines were less dictatorial about women's

10. *Princess Alice in her wedding gown of white lace, over a crinoline petticoat with a white lace veil, in 1862. She had orange blossom in her hair and round the hem of her petticoat.*

11. *The Prince and Princess of Wales. Edward and Alexandra were married at St George's Chapel, Windsor, in 1863. The Prince wore the uniform of an army general, the scarlet of his tunic hardly visible under the voluminous blue velvet mantle of a Knight of the Garter. The Princess wore her flower-trimmed satin and tulle dress over layers of petticoats, in preference to the fashionable cage crinoline, which she was said to dislike.*

wedding dresses, which were normally made in the current
fashion for day dresses and worn with either a bonnet or a veil
hanging behind the head. Orange blossom was used to trim the
bonnet or worn as a wreath over the veil. By the end of the
decade some brides were entering church with their veils over
their faces. Veils and orange blossom could be worn with either a
white or a coloured dress. Brides of social standing wore white, as
did their bridesmaids, so that in some 1860s wedding groups it is
often difficult at first glance to pick out the bride, but many young
women of the lower middle or artisan class simply had a new best,
coloured dress. Since the Victorians seemed to spend so much
time in mourning (a then universal social convention with very
strict rules), many wedding dresses were grey or lavender
coloured, both considered suitable colours for half mourning.

In the early 1860s most wedding dresses, whatever their colour,
were of silk taffeta, with full gathered skirts worn over a crinoline
petticoat that from the side resembled a right-angled triangle,
being fairly straight in the front but sweeping out behind. The
bodices of these dresses were close fitting, with high, round
necklines. The sleeves were long, moderately fitted and cut with
two seams to give a curved line. Compared with the flounced,
lower necked, shorter or wider sleeved dresses worn over
bell-shaped crinolines of the 1850s, they were plain almost to
severity, although they were often trimmed with silk fringing to
give a yoke effect on the bodice.

The fabrics of the dresses from this decade that survive in
museums are superbly beautiful, whether they are of plain
taffeta, softly muted stripes or small, all-over, self-colour,
bordered diaper patterns. The silk has a soft sheen. By 1867 the
simplicity of style began to change and a fashion magazine
advised summer brides: 'White book-muslins have, in a measure,
superseded the heavy satins and silks. They are profusely trained,
with puffings divided by sections of lace, and are *en tablier* or
simulating an open overskirt.'

Princess Alice, in 1861, had worn a plainly cut lace dress over a
crinoline petticoat, but her sister-in-law, Princess Alexandra,
wore a highly decorated dress festooned with wreaths of orange
blossom and myrtle between swathes of tulle and lace for her
marriage to the Prince of Wales in 1863. He was the last royal
bridegroom to wear the mantle of a Knight of the Garter over his
wedding clothes. His bride was attended by eight bridesmaids
dressed in white tulle festooned with blush roses, shamrocks and
heather. They also wore veils, falling over the backs of their

12. *On his twenty-third birthday, 7th January 1865, John Mayall married sixteen-year-old Eliza Dabbs at the parish church at Lancing, West Sussex. Her father was the local innkeeper and John came from a well known family of Victorian photographers, who had studios in London and Brighton. After the wedding the young couple were photographed at the Mayall studio in Brighton, probably by the bridegroom's father or another member of the family. John wore dark trousers and frock coat (possibly blue) and carried a black top hat. Eliza wore a white silk dress over a crinoline petticoat, a white veil, and a dark blue velvet jacket edged with fur or swansdown. She wore a wreath of artificial orange blossom in her hair and appears to be carrying a large lace handkerchief.*

13. *An unknown bridal group in a garden, taken, probably in 1869, by T. Andrews, photographer, of High Street, Epsom. The groom wore dark clothes, which contrast starkly with the white dresses of the bride and bridesmaids. The bride's dress hangs stiffly over her crinoline and was probably of satin or even white grosgrain silk taffeta. The bridesmaids' dresses are of a lighter weight fabric, possibly tulle, and have at least five rows of small frills round the hem. Note the shape of the crinoline of the bridesmaid on the left: it is flatter in front and longer behind than that of Eliza Mayall in picture 12.*

heads from wreaths of the same flowers that trimmed their dresses. The comment was made of many of the Victorian royal brides that they were 'sunk in the greenery' and resembled walking flower gardens. Those who could afford to made their weddings as much like the royal ones as possible, complete with a train of bridesmaids, and sometimes as many colourful grooms-men to attend the groom. For summer weddings marquees were set up in gardens and decorated with flowers. Middle-class families made as much of a celebration as they could and younger sisters acted as bridesmaids. However, wedding photographs and surviving dresses from the 1860s show that few brides were festooned with flowers like Princess Alexandra. Even in 1869, some of them followed Princess Alice's example of a plainly cut dress over a crinoline petticoat.

Growing sophistication, 1870-90

The crinoline petticoat disappeared from fashionable wear in the late 1860s, but the wide voluminous skirts, fuller in the back than the front, remained. In the 1870s these skirts were swathed up behind the woman's body and became complicated short trains held out at the back by a crinolette or bustle. This was a petticoat whose back portion only was stiffened with rows of horsehair frills. The bustle was to remain popular for nearly

14. *Princess Louise, in a bustled dress of 1871, with a long court train, was married to the Marquis of Lorne on 21st March 1871. By this time the wide hooped crinoline petticoat had gone out of fashion and a narrower line was considered more elegant in which the dress was held out at the back only by rows of horsehair frills. In 1871 a petticoat called the 'Princess Louise crinoline' was advertised as doing away with 'the unsightly results of the ordinary hoops'.*

15. *A carte-de-visite by Henry Banger of King Street, Richmond, inscribed on the back in an unknown hand 'Amy as a bridesmaid 1874'. She wears a bustle dress, probably silk, trimmed with velvet ribbon, and carries a basket of flowers. Her dress is fairly dark in colour, but the bride she attended may well not have worn a white dress. The turban-like 'head-dress' is, in fact, a thick plait of false hair set with an ornament. Amy is very fashionable, for in the early years of the 1870s more false hair was worn than in any other decade of the nineteenth century. Because of this women often went without hats. When hats reappeared at the end of the 1870s they were either turbans that followed the shape of the earlier hairstyles or flat plates tipped well forward over the eyes to leave room for the coils of hair behind them. (See page 22, picture 17.)*

twenty years although in two distinct styles separated by a couple of years (about 1880) when it disappeared altogether in favour of very tight hobble skirts that were neither universally popular nor universally worn. The fashion magazines' advice to the 1870s bride was that wedding dresses should be 'in the style of a fashionably trained toilette'. Princess Louise, Victoria's fourth daughter, chose an evening dress style for her wedding to the Marquis of Lorne in 1871. For white weddings the popular fabric was a rich creamy satin. Ivory, rather than dead white, was to be popular for wedding dresses for the next fifty years. Many of these ivory dresses were altered for evening wear afterwards.

A 'trained toilette' could mean a day dress, for these too had trains in the 1870s. Some of these dresses consisted of a skirt long

16. *Thomas Bridger was a blacksmith and wheelwright of Kingston upon Thames. He was a staunch chapelgoer, joint founder of the Sunday school at the Norbiton Primitive Methodist church. Here he is pictured after his wedding to his second wife, Sarah, in 1877. He wore his best, dark suit with two watch chains across his high-buttoning waistcoat. She wore a fitted dress, probably with a small bustle, in two colours of silk and velvet. She, too, had a watch chain, her 'lady's watch' being tucked into a little pocket made at the waist of her dress for this purpose. The chain was taken across her bodice and pinned or passed through a buttonhole on the left-hand side. She also wore a small lace-edged scarf, and her dress was trimmed with two rows of buttons from neck to knee. Her sleeves were tucked in rows across the top and had velvet forearms with small turnback cuffs of silk, edged inside the sleeve with a narrow lace. This would have been a very fashionable dress at the time and she doubtless wore it for several years as her best dress.*

17. *A wedding group taken in the Reeves Studio at Lewes, East Sussex, in August 1877. The bride wears a white dress trimmed with a small 'Elizabethan' ruff at the neck; the bodice of her dress has a chevron-pleated front panel. The rest of her dress appears very plain but close examination shows that there is ruching at the hem and she has a train that is gathered in flounced bands. Her small flower-spray head-dress is set very far back on her neatly parted hair. The bridesmaids, seated in front, wear very fashionable light-coloured dresses trimmed with a darker, contrasting colour; their trains are ruched and banded with ribbon and pleated frills, as are the cuffs of their sleeves. They have wide-brimmed 'Dolly Varden' straw hats trimmed with ostrich feathers and tipped forward over their foreheads, in contrast to most of the other women in the picture, who wear the more typical 1870s turban-like hat. All the women carry flowers as well as wearing flowers pinned to their dresses. All the men wear dark, probably black coats, although it is not possible to make out the style. The bridegroom and the bride's father wear light-coloured trousers, and all the men, with one exception, wear white bow ties or cravats.*

enough to trail on the ground at the back and worn under a shorter skirt attached to the bodice. This overskirt was looped up at the back by means of tapes tied inside it to form the soft bustle of the early and mid 1870s. Sometimes an apron front with a frill all round its edge was added. Wedding dresses in this style survive in several museums. Most of them are of taffeta in a wide variety of colours and often trimmed with black or brown lace or braid.

At the end of the 1870s the bustle was discarded for a while. Dresses were made in one piece, closely fitted and panelled down to the hips, where swathes of material were draped across the front to fall at the back with a train. Sometimes the swathing was formed by gathering the centre front seam of the skirt for much of its length, the material then being stitched in small unpressed pleats into the side seams. These close fitting dresses were known as 'cuirass dresses' and a dark grey silk example, recorded as a wedding dress of 1879, survives in Weybridge Museum. The cuirass dresses became narrower and narrower in the last year of the decade and in 1880 the train was discarded as well as the bustle. But the very tight skirt was not popular, and in 1881 the bustle returned, although not the long train. The 1880s bustle was higher and harder; it often consisted of a small cushion pad tied

18. *Another photograph from the Reeves Studio, taken in a garden sometime in 1879/80, presents a fascinating cross-section of generations at a somewhat less formal Victorian wedding. The bride, seated centre, in a mid-tone dress with white lace at the neck and cuffs, appears much older than her two bridesmaids in their light-coloured dresses with cuirass bodices and four-tiered skirts. Although all the women in the photograph wear fairly narrow skirts, clear of the ground and untrained (typical of 1880), their accessories range from the fashions of several years. The three elderly women wear the brimless turban hats of the mid 1870s, while the bridesmaids and the other two women wear the newest brimmed hats, heralding the fashions of the next thirty years in which hats grew gradually larger and wider. The men, too, wear a mixture of styles, the older ones in frock coats and the younger in morning coats, while the man sitting on the garden chair at the front of the picture appears to be wearing a lounge jacket.*

19. *Miss Christina Gibson, daughter of a Leith fish merchant, was married to Donald Gray, a fish curer, at Leith on 16th April 1885. She wore a cream satin dress with a long, separate train fastened at the waist of her very fashionable bustle dress. This dress is now in Barcaldine Castle Museum, at Benderloch, Argyll, Scotland. It has a close-fitting bodice, high to the throat, with a small turndown collar, and the plain sleeves that, either long or elbow-length, were typical of the 1880s. The photograph, taken by Wood and Company, of 72 Princes Street, Edinburgh, shows how short (well clear of the shoe) the lace-trimmed skirt was.*

on to the waist at the back. This was worn under a skirt that was flat in front but heavily pleated and long enough at the back to give an even hem all round well clear of the ground and often revealing the shoes or boots. On top of the skirt was an apron-like swathe of material that was pulled up to drape over the bustle at the back, where it stuck out like a little shelf at the waist.

The pastel colours of the 1860s were superseded in the 1870s and 1880s by the newly discovered aniline dyes. Some of the colours seem startling for wedding dresses. The Welsh Folk Museum has a wedding dress of 1875 in bronze taffeta; the

Merseyside County Museum has a claret coloured velvet and satin wedding dress of 1879 and a deep amethyst purple dress of 1880, also described as a wedding dress. Two other 1880s wedding dresses in this museum are purplish brown satin with an overskirt and trimmings of copper coloured brocade, worn by the bride of a farmer in 1884, and a grey corded silk dress of 1886. They are all walking length and the 1880s dresses have no trains. For a white wedding the style was often the same, but an extra piece of material was added at the back of the waist to form a train.

The custom of having small children, especially little boys, as train bearers seems to have become popular in the 1880s. They were often put into various forms of fancy dress for the occasion, a custom that has been perpetuated ever since. Kilted Scotsmen or 'Little Lord Fauntleroy' outfits were probably the most common. While 1860s bridesmaids had worn white like the bride, those of the 1870s and 1880s provided a colourful contrast. Even royalty broke its own convention of white for bridesmaids in 1889 when a second Princess Louise, the daughter of the Prince of Wales, dressed her bridesmaids in blush pink. They carried pink roses and wore wreaths of similar roses in their hair. In the same year the *Surrey Advertiser* reported the wedding of a schoolmistress on 31st December under the heading 'A most interesting marriage': 'At St Matthew's Church, Surbiton, Miss Amelia Alexander of St Matthew's School and Mr F. R. Stanford of Tolworth. The bride wore a dress of light claret silk with a wreath and veil, and carried a handsome bouquet, the gift of the bridegroom. Her two elder bridesmaids wore grey silk, trimmed with moire, the two younger were dressed in crushed strawberry colour. All four carried baskets of white flowers and maidenhair fern.'

One of the reasons for the many coloured wedding dresses worn in the late 1880s and the 1890s is the change in the canonical hours in 1886, which made afternoon weddings popular. A fashion magazine of the following year commented: 'Afternoon weddings have caused a great reform; a bride is often married in her going-away dress.'

But as brides and bridesmaids became more colourful the bridegroom gradually became more sombre. The blue frock coats and pale trousers of the 1860s were still worn at white weddings of the 1870s, but in the 1880s the morning coat became popular. These coats were cut away in front from the waist, although, like the frock coat, they were worn just above the knee at the back.

20 (opposite). *Nessie Muspratt was the second daughter of Edmund Muspratt, head of Muspratt Chemical Works and chairman of the United Alkali Company (which later became part of ICI). The Muspratt family were supporters of the Liberal Party, and after her marriage to Egerton Stewart-Brown in September 1888 Nessie took up a local political career, being the first woman to speak on a municipal platform when her husband stood for Liverpool City Council in 1892. She was a keen suffragist and went on to become the chairman or president of several women's Liberal councils. She was the second woman elected to Liverpool City Council in 1919 and for many years was a well-known justice of the peace, retiring from public life in 1938. For her wedding dress she chose a close-fitting fashionable design in pearl grey and silver satin brocade, with a high neck and three-quarter sleeves. The gored skirt was narrow in front but swept out behind to a train over a small pad bustle; a longer overtrain was added at the waist. Although similar in style to the dress worn by Christina Gray (picture 19), it was longer and the bustle was smaller and flatter. The dress was trimmed with four bunches of orange blossom and bows of satin ribbon, and the veil was large and long. The dress was made in Liverpool by Jane Merrick of Rodney Street and the photograph was from the studio of Barrand in Bold Street. Both are now in the Merseyside County Museums costume collections.*

21 (right). *A photographically produced cabinet print of a sketch of a bridal couple 'alone at last'. This is one of a pair; the other, with another poem, depicts them on the following morning. The bride in this sketch is wearing the plainly cut dress of the late 1880s with long tight sleeves, buttoned on the forearm, and a plain skirt with a frill at the bottom, the skirt lengthening behind to form a short train. Her veil is long, billowing over the dress. Her bridegroom is wearing evening dress with a cut-away 'swallow tail' coat. This would not normally be worn for a wedding, but if an afternoon wedding was followed by a dance at which the young couple were present, the groom might well change his clothes, even if the bride did not. The verse reads:*

*At last the wedding guests are gone
And lip to lip the happy pair
Sit trembling, waiting for the hour
Which consummates their greatest
    bliss.*

*What in hours of sweetest fancies
In moments of pure happiness
Oft they dreamt, and oft they
    longed for
Is reality at last.*

*And the veil, in sweet caresses,
Yields to love's most ardent touch;
Gently then they draw the curtain
To hide love's secret with a blush.*

In the twentieth century all this may be thought very coy, but the Victorians collected such cards with enthusiasm.

THE NIGHT OF THE WEDDING.

The morning coats were either dark blue or black, worn with grey trousers and tie and a white waistcoat. The *Tailor and Cutter* lamented that 'there is no set style nowadays' but the fashionable Victorian gentleman and many others below him in the social scale were bound as tightly by fashion as their womenfolk. The wearing of morning coats to weddings and other functions was of short duration; by the 1890s the frock coat was back in fashion, but it had lost the last of its colour and was acceptable only in black.

Confidence and opulence, 1890-1900

Until the 1880s countrymen, craftsmen, artisans and labourers had not worn 'fashionable' clothes. Their basic outfits were

22. *The Victorian interest in collecting pictures of weddings is shown again in this card by Valentines of Dundee. It is one of a pair depicting fisherfolk weddings in Auchmithie, a small fishing village on the Scottish east coast. Auchmithie is just north of Arbroath and is the original home of the kippers known as Arbroath smokies. This card shows the bridal pair, their friends and families on parade through the village street, led by the local fiddler. The bride wears a dark two-piece dress, with a white collar; her bridegroom wears a dark suit with a double-breasted waistcoat, a top hat and a white scarf folded round his neck in place of a collar and tie. The other card, not reproduced here, shows a bride in a white dress and a groom in a dark suit, white scarf and top hat. Neither bride has any kind of head-dress or flowers. Their clothes are in the style that would have been considered fashionable best wear in the village community. Although a commercial card, this is probably an accurate representation of the local custom of walking to and from the church for a wedding.*

23 (above). *A wedding group at Holystone, Northumberland, photographed about 1890, by W. S. Hubbard, photographer, of Barlborough in Derbyshire. This group of people are on their way to the next village for the wedding (Holystone church was not licensed for marriages at the time). They pose under a wych elm (which still survives) by the wall of Holystone churchyard. The picture presents the puzzle 'Which are the bride and groom?' There are two possibilities: either the young couple in the centre of the group, the boy with his gloved hand on the girl's shoulder, or the older couple fourth and fifth from the left of the group. It is an interesting and genuine picture of country people in their best clothes, dressed for a wedding.*

24 (right). *A wistful bride who was married at Rostherne church, Knutsford, Cheshire, on 17th September 1890. This dress is of cream satin, trimmed with lace, and has a centre back skirt panel forming the train of figured silk and silver thread. Like the dresses of the royal brides, it is trimmed with white artificial orange blossom and green leaves. The dress was later altered by lowering the neckline and shortening the sleeves for wear as an evening dress, and in this state it survives, together with its wearer's photograph, in the Gallery of English Costume, Manchester. The ideal woman of 1890 had a very small waist, and the photographer has drastically retouched the negative to make the waist appear unnaturally small.*

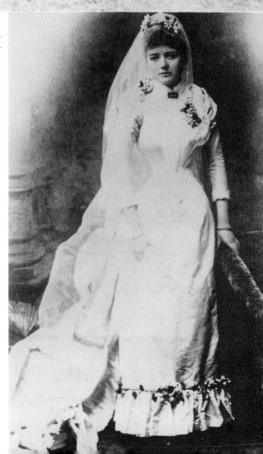

straight-legged trousers, usually of a light colour, a shirt and a waistcoat. In many kinds of active work a jacket was never worn, but for leisure and colder days they had a close fitting jacket with high set lapels and rounded lower front edges. These garments, made in a variety of sturdy fabrics and dull colours, had been worn by workers in a wide range of occupations from the 1830s onward. For their wedding they would have a new set of clothes in their normal style. If they kept it for best it would have lasted the rest of their life. Some countrymen were married in white smocks in the early or mid nineteenth century, and some of these are now preserved in museums, recorded as 'wedding smocks'. By the 1880s the 'lounge suit', based on the cut of the working man's clothes, but made in lighter weight fabrics, had become fashionable casual wear for gentlemen. They would certainly not have worn such a suit to a wedding, but the workers took up the lounge suit for best wear and among them it became a wedding suit.

Gertrude Jekyll, recording the changes of the country people in west Surrey at the turn of the nineteenth and twentieth centuries, deplored this hankering for 'fashion' by working folk and wrote: 'A lamentable example was shown me lately. It was a photograph of a wedding party of the labouring class. The bride had a veil and orange blossom, a shower bouquet and *pages*. The bridegroom wore one of those cheap suits aforesaid and had a billycock hat pushed back from his poor anxious excited face that glistened with sweat. In his buttonhole was a large bouquet and on his

25 (opposite). *A page from the 'Lady's Pictorial' for 23rd July 1892, featuring the wedding dress and going-away dress of Miss Ethel Reiss, eldest daughter of Mr J. E. Reiss of Joddrell Hall, Holmes Chapel, Cheshire, who married Captain Donne of the 6th Dragoon Guards (Carabiniers) on 14th July 1892. The wedding was reported in several newspapers as well as the 'Lady's Pictorial'. The description of the bride's dress is straightforward: 'a dress of rich white satin, the petticoat and bodice being elaborately trimmed with old Brussels lace; the train which fell from her shoulders was of brocade. She wore a tulle veil over a wreath of orange blossom fastened by a diamond crescent and she carried a bouquet of choice white flowers.' However, the description of the bridesmaids' dresses (bottom right of the picture) is highly amusing. According to one of the newspaper reports, they wore 'rich cream surah dresses, sweetly fashioned with seamless bodice and short rucked sleeves, pelerine of antique lace and handsome ceinture of satin ribbon finished with bows at the back. Their large picturesque hats were composed of old lace with black velvet pot à fleurs renversé crown, trimmed with black plumes and pink roses; and narrow velvet strings attached with diamond pins. They carried shower bouquets of pink roses.' To translate, short, for sleeves in the 1890s, meant elbow length, surah is a soft twilled silk fabric, a pelerine is a very short shoulder cape, a ceinture is a sash, and, if you can afford to fasten the strings of your hat with diamond pins, perhaps it does not matter if its crown is described in dressmaker's French as 'a flower pot upside down'. The newspaper reports also described the going-away dress (top right of picture), the wedding presents and several of the bride's trousseau dresses. These latter were also illustrated in the 'Lady's Pictorial'.*

26. *A photograph of Lady Edith Ward in her bridal dress (left), published in a weekly newspaper in 1894 after her marriage to Lord Woverton. This wedding was reported in several newspapers, which all showed the portrait picture of Lady Edith (above), taken by Alice Hughes of Gower Street, a well known lady photographer of the 1890s. Lady Edith's 'leg of mutton' sleeved wedding dress was trimmed with orange blossom and leaves.*

hands *white cotton gloves*. No more pitiful exhibition would well be imagined. Have these poor people so utterly lost the sense of the dignity of their own position that they can derive satisfaction from the performance of such an absurd burlesque?' The couple concerned, however, were probably proud of the photograph. But while the country and working man confidently followed the fashions set by the middle class, that same middle class was collecting postcards and photographs of the 'picturesque' country folk. 'Staged' weddings in remote districts showing unusual customs or strange clothes were very popular subjects.

Any man who employed other men would have counted himself above the working class and would have worn for a wedding clothes as close to those of a gentleman as he could. In such a case not only the groom but the best man, the fathers of the bride and groom and all the male guests would have worn the 'uniform' of black frock coat faced with silk over grey trousers

27. *An 1894 photograph from the family album of the Annetts, master traders in Walton-on-Thames. The bride wore a coloured two-piece dress with a cream or white plastron fronted bodice. The dress itself is decorated with braid embroidery and is closely moulded to the figure. Unlike the society brides, this girl's skirt probably had no more than a very small train to the back of the skirt. She wore a large 'two yards square' veil and orange blossom. Her bridegroom wore a slightly unfashionable morning coat, for the frock coat came back into favour during the 1890s, having been replaced by the morning coat in the 1880s.*

28. *A working class bride and groom from St Helens, Merseyside, about 1896. The young bride worked for the photographers Jordan and Metcalfe, and her employers took a portrait of the young couple after the wedding. The groom wore a morning suit, not a lounge suit; he was probably a tradesman or clerk, not a labourer. The bride wore a light-coloured going-away dress, and a wide-brimmed straw hat lavishly trimmed with tulle. Her blouse and scarf were of lace and her bouquet was tied with white ribbon. Gloves were normally worn with all outdoor clothes, but the dark leather gloves worn by this bride strike an odd note. (Right). The very elegant back of the cabinet print showing the photographer's name.*

with either a light coloured waistcoat and a dark tie, or a dark coloured waistcoat and a light tie. Shirts were invariably white and a grey top hat completed the outfit. Dull though it sounds, the same colour scheme is still fashionable in the 1980s and many would argue that it forms the perfect foil for the white dress of the bride and the colours of the bridesmaids and women guests.

Fashionable women's clothes of the 1890s, including wedding

dresses, were very elaborate. Ladies' dresses, to judge by the newspapers of the time, were subjects of immense interest and discussion. Almost every report of society events in the decade, from court presentations to weddings and christenings, local fetes or 'at homes' and race meetings, listed people present and described in detail the clothes worn by the ladies. Late Victorian journalists often used the word 'simple' for dresses which seem to us to be very overdecorated. Yet in comparison to the intricately draped skirts of the 1870s and 1880s those of the 1890s are very plainly cut, being narrow over the waist, smoothly fitting over the hips and hanging straight to the floor in front, with any fullness taken to the back, where, the bustle being abandoned, the hem generally trailed a little on the ground. The decoration had moved upwards and the fashionable bodices of the 1890s were very elaborate.

29. James Fenton, a calico printer, married Mary Laycock at Littleborough on 10th June 1897. It was the year of Queen Victoria's Diamond Jubilee and Mary wore a white lace 'Jubilee bonnet' for her wedding, fastening her wreath of orange blossom inside the brim and tying the ribbons beneath her chin. She wore no veil and her dress was a smart tailored two-piece in a pastel colour. The leg of mutton sleeves of the early 1890s had become close-fitting long sleeves with a short puffed sleeve at the shoulder, and all the women in the front row, as well as the child, wore this type of sleeve. The men wore morning style suits. The bride's father and the bridegroom wore bowler hats while the groom's father wore a top hat. The photograph of the wedding party was taken in the street near the bride's home.

30. *Wedding dress and court dress. Miss Charlotte Dougall was married to Mr Arthur Meadows-White on 22nd April 1897. For her wedding she wore a dress of ivory satin with a full court train from the shoulders. After the wedding she was presented at court again as a married woman and for this presentation she wore her wedding dress again but with the high collar and yoke and the narrow undersleeves removed. This studio portrait, which appeared later in the year as the frontispiece to a national magazine, shows the bodice and train of her wedding dress, worn with an embroidered skirt, long white gloves and court feathers.*

31. *The small atten-dant at the wedding of Miss Henrietta Cald-well to Captain E. A. E. Bulwar of the 1st South Staffordshire Regiment at St John the Baptist church, Wimbledon, in June 1899 was dressed as a miniature drummer boy in a red and gold copy of an early eight-eenth-century army uniform. However, he had the up-to-date 'VR' in his hat, for Queen Victoria was still on the throne. The bridegroom and his best man, a fellow officer, both wore black frock coats over grey trousers. The bride wore a white satin and brocade dress trimmed with old Irish lace and fes-tooned with orange blossom and leaves. The six bridesmaids wore dresses of pale grey voile with cape collars embroidered with braid. They also wore red straw and chiffon hats trimmed with cherries and car-ried bouquets of red carnations.*

From 1890 to 1895 the tops of women's sleeves became larger and larger; these are the 'leg of mutton' sleeves. After 1895 the sleeve could be in two parts, a long close fitting sleeve with a large puffed oversleeve covering the top of the arm. This puff became small towards 1900 but double (short over long) sleeves were still worn. Vertical tucks, folded or pouched panels on the bodice fronts and swathed sashes around very tight waists were popular in a variety of materials. An alternative to the vertical front panel was the yoked effect, either square or oval, trimmed and emphasised with frills of chiffon or lace. This was very widely used in the second half of the decade. The neckline of day dresses was invariably high and if the line of the dress was low then a lace, or chiffon chemisette was worn under it to give a high, close fitting, boned upstanding collar. Society brides almost always chose an ivory colour, described in the newspaper as 'white', for their wedding dresses.

Many society brides were presented or re-presented at court after their marriage and in the second half of the decade it became the custom to wear the wedding dress again for this occasion. As court etiquette demanded low necklines and short sleeves for the presentation, at the wedding the separate chemisette with high neck and long sleeves was worn under the court dress. The skirts of the dresses were cut long and flowing at the back, making a train that could be held up in the hand for dancing. For the court presentation a full-length court train, rather like a cloak, was added to the shoulders of the dress.

Such a train could be part of a wedding dress and this would need small attendants to carry it in the church. These children, usually boys, could be dressed in any style at all, so long as it covered the child completely (no bare arms or legs). They were often very elaborately dressed in copies of military uniform or historic costume, as ornate as the child could be persuaded to wear. Bridesmaids wore stylish day dresses in whatever colour the bride decreed. They were usually dressed alike, or matched in twos. There might be any number up to eight. In place of the wreaths, veils and bonnets of the previous decades elaborately decorated hats were perched on top of piled-up hair. In 1897 a brief vogue for 'Jubilee' bonnets occurred, and some were worn by bridesmaids, or even brides, but hats were the normal headwear for all women. Only the bride wore a veil, and even this was to be a variable fashion after 1900.

3. The grand Edwardian occasion, 1901-13

With the coronation of King Edward VII fashion took a lighter, more frivolous turn. Britain had plunged into mourning for Queen Victoria, but with her had died some of the restraints of her reign, and when the mourning period was over lighter fabrics and softer fashions were worn for wedding dresses as for other occasions. The heavy satin skirts with bodices trimmed with stiff frills of the 1890s were replaced by lace and chiffon, fine ninon and soft velvet ensembles that draped gracefully over the new S-shaped corset of the fashionable bride. Many brides wore hats, rather than veils, but where veils were worn they were usually waist length and were held well back on the top of the head with a wreath of flowers. Cream and ivory were popular colours for wedding dresses, which often had a bewildering variety of fabrics incorporated into the same dress. This mixing of fabrics was to continue into the 1920s. The society woman's custom of wearing the wedding dress again for her court presentation continued and this influenced wedding fashions up to 1913. Many brides who were never likely to be presented at court wore low-cut, draped necklines to their gowns over a lace or chiffon chemisette as in the previous decade. The dress bodices pouched at the waist in front and the skirts floated to trail on the floor at the back. The huge stiff sleeves of the 1890s disappeared and three-quarter length sleeves became acceptable.

Alongside this increasing softness in Edwardian dress a different look for women had become fashionable; this was the tailored suit, consisting of a 'walking length' skirt, clear of the ground all round, a fitted jacket and a blouse. The blouse was often heavily frilled, with a high neck, and the jacket was sometimes decorated with braid and buttons, but the general effect was neat and practical. Either style could be worn by the same woman on differing occasions. In the early 1900s few fashionable women would have chosen a tailored suit as a wedding dress, but servant girls or working-class brides sometimes wore a suit that afterwards could become best wear. When clothes are few and expensive a suit and lacy blouse are a better investment than a dress.

In 1900 the black frock coat was the correct formal dress for men, worn with grey striped trousers and a light waistcoat. During the next decade the frock coat was gradually ousted by

32. *Charles Anning was a young Londoner who joined the Metropolitan Police Force on 1st January 1900. He was the first man in the force to be issued with a bicycle. On 13th August 1904 he married Maud Mercer (a London girl, from Bow) at St George's church, Hanover Square. He wore a black frock coat and trousers, and a shirt with a stiff turnover collar. Maud wore a white ninon dress with a deep cape-like frill cascading from a lace-trimmed round yoke and falling over full sleeves that were gathered at the elbow as well as the wrist. Her skirt was a new style circular skirt, sunray pleated into the waistband, and cut some 4 inches (100 mm) longer at the back than the front. Her veil was the same 'two yards square' with a hand-stitched hem that had been fashionable from the mid 1890s (see picture 27).*

the morning coat, although the frock coat could still be correct wedding attire up to the outbreak of the First World War. The higher up the social scale the young couple were the less choice they had in what they could wear. Convention ruled most people's lives very strictly until 1914 and weddings were very conventional occasions. Tradesmen wore morning coats (frock coats if they were wealthy) and working men wore lounge suits. Foreigners, especially Americans or Germans, sometimes wore lounge suits at weddings in England but by anyone with social pretensions this would have been considered 'ungentlemanly'.

While brides' dresses were often altered to evening dresses after the wedding, bridesmaids' dresses were made as fashionable 'day dress' or 'afternoon dress' styles. In the early years of the twentieth century bridesmaids wore pouched fronted bodices with boleros or bolero effects, double sleeves or three-quarter sleeves, long skirts and very large hats. Their dresses were made in two pieces, the waistband of the bodice overlying that of the skirt, where they were held together with hooks and eyes. One-piece 'princess' style dresses with no waist seam or 'Empire line' dresses with a seam under the bust were popular after 1907. Necklines were always high. Not until 1909 did a lower neckline become acceptable for day wear and even then it was considered outrageous by many. The lower neckline, usually a small turn-down collar, first appeared on blouses. By 1910 'costumes', or softer, more decorated versions of the tailored suit, perhaps worn with such a blouse, can be seen in wedding photographs, worn by bridesmaids.

33. *The wedding group of Lottie Allam and Charles Farlay is pictured in a garden setting at Marlow, Buckinghamshire, in 1904. The bride was one of six children and her four sisters, Louisa, Nellie, Sarah and Grace, were her bridesmaids. Also in the picture is her brother William and a brother-in-law, Harry Childs. The gentlemen wore black frock coats and trousers, double-breasted roll-collared waistcoats with watch chains, high stiff collars and top hats. Like so many Edwardian young men, they all had moustaches. The bride wore a white tailored-style wedding dress with a wide collar held by a strap across a softly pleated and pouched front panel to the bodice. Her sleeves were plain and tight fitting while her slightly trained skirt had two tucks near the bottom. The bridesmaids also wore tailor-made pastel or white dresses, also with wide collars and plain long sleeves. Like the bride, they all wore high collared chemisettes under their dresses, the collar fastened in front with a small bar brooch. Such brooches were often given by the groom as a present to the bridesmaids. Their collars are plain, but the bride's collar is finished at the top with a small frill like a miniature Elizabethan ruff.*

34 (above). *An unknown bridal group from the Malvern district poses in a backyard after the wedding. The bride wears a light-coloured (possibly cream) suit, a lace blouse with a high boned collar, and a large hat festooned with lace trimmings; with this outfit she wears black stockings and shoes. Her two bridesmaids wear coloured ankle-length tailored suits, lacy blouses and equally large flower-trimmed hats. The date is probably about 1908, for in that year there was a brief return to the fashion of pleating the tops of sleeves into the armhole of a jacket, reminiscent of the 1890s. In 1908, too, hats became bigger and finally lost the little veils which had dangled at eye level on many women's hats since the early years of the century. All three women carry a fashionably large bouquet. The bridegroom sits stiffly in his best dark suit and high starched collar. He carries his gloves in his hands, but neither he nor the other men in the group have hats.*

36 (right). *On 2nd September 1909 Polly Chadwick married Herbert Blakeley at Leeds. Their families were photographed together on the steps of the Chadwicks' home in Portland Crescent. The bride wore a white dress with a high collar and long sleeves. (In style it was similar to the dresses shown on the front cover and in picture 37.) The bridegroom wore a dark suit. The bridesmaids, who were the respective sisters of the bride and groom, wore cream serge skirts and jackets edged with coffee-coloured braid over blouses with lace-edged collars. These costumes were very fashionable for they were the just above the shoe length increasingly popular with younger women (who showed neat black shoes and stockings with confidence) but were more softly styled than the normal tailored suit (see 34). With these costumes they wore black straw hats trimmed with ostrich plumes. The small attendants were the children of the bride's elder sister and both were dressed in cream serge, the little girl with a cream straw and lace bonnet, the boy with a round sailor type cap. The bride's father, at the right of the picture, wore a frock coat, and the bridegroom's mother, on the left of the front row, carried a bouquet of flowers. This was not uncommon and in some Edwardian photographs both bride's and groom's mothers have bouquets as well as the bride and bridesmaids. At this wedding, however, although the child bridesmaid had a bouquet, the two older ones did not. The picture shows several women in the tucked sleeves which were so popular in the period 1908-12. The smooth shoulder line was more fashionable in 1909 than the gathered or pleated sleeve head which characterised new clothes of 1908.*

35 (above). *In 1908 a junior minister, the Reverend Philip Evans, was appointed to the Primitive Methodist church at Kingston upon Thames. During his term of office he married, in 1908, one of his congregation, Miss Rose Gosford of Norbiton. Rose was one of a large family and this picture shows them grouped in a garden. Rose sat in the centre wearing a white dress and veil with her bridesmaids on each side of her. All of them have four deep tucks round the hem of their dresses, including the youngest bridesmaid, whose dress is only mid-calf length. The bridesmaids wore new, fashionably large hats, while the other women in the group had slightly smaller hats. Philip Evans stood behind his bride and wore his 'uniform' of dark clerical grey suit, black back-fastening waistcoat and white clerical collar. He was the only man in the group not wearing a tie but none of them wore hats.*

The menu reads:

Menu

Lobster Cutlets.
Tomatoe Sauce.
Roast Chicken.
Ham. Tongue.
Salad.
Roast Sirloin Beef.
Jellies & Creams.
Meringues.
French Pastry.
Cheese. Butter. Rolls.
Dessert.
Coffee.

37. *When Ethel Smith married William Taylor at St Mark's church, Surbiton, in 1910 (see picture on front cover) she was attended by four bridesmaids, two adults and two little girls. One each of these is shown in the picture. The wedding was reported in the local paper in great detail: 'The first two (bridesmaids) were attired in Princesse costumes of ivory cloth with soutache trimmings, black hats, and wore enamel pendant watches, the gift of the bridegroom. The Misses Coochey wore dainty dresses of cream-striped delaine and large cream silk hats, and wore gold chains and pendants, the gift of the bridegroom. Each bridesmaid carried a floral horseshoe composed of pink hyacinths and carnations with trails of similax. The bride's mother wore a costume of mulberry chiffon, with hat to match.' (Soutache was a narrow braid; delaine was a soft wool fabric.) The older bridesmaids' dresses had the fashionably tucked sleeves and were given a slightly military air by the two rows of buttons and the cream-coloured braid on the cream cloth. They wore their watches pinned on the left. The little girls' dresses were tucked round the hem and worn over black shoes and stockings. It sounds a very pretty wedding, with the usual colourings reversed as the bride wore hyacinth blue. The wedding 'breakfast', which was a full scale lunch, was held at the home of a friend, and a handwritten menu was provided. The addresses of both bride and groom, and that of the friend, were given in the newspaper; all were houses which would have kept at least two or three servants at that time. The bridegroom was as generous as his father-in-law's friend, for his wedding gift to his bride was a full set of fitch furs which she wore with her going-away coat and skirt of Parma violet, together with a black hat trimmed with black satin and feathers.*

38. *A charming photograph of an unknown bride and groom in a back garden, standing on a straw mat. The studious-looking young groom wore a morning suit with a pale grey waistcoat, while his bride wore a white or cream version of Mrs Taylor's dress (see front cover). This dress had plain fitted sleeves with three tucks in the upper arm; a draped bodice, finished with a flat bow, over a plain high neck; and a plain front panel to the skirt, with two tucks in the side panels. The back of the skirt had a slight train. Her veil was held in place by a wreath of flowers, probably orange blossom, and she carried a shower bouquet.*

39 (left). 'Three pretty trainbearers' was the heading of the newspaper report to accompany this picture of the little attendants on Miss Phyllis Green when she married the eminent soldier Lieutenant George Milner, DSO, commander of the 5th Royal Irish Lancers, at St George's church, Hanover Square, in 1910. The companion photograph shows no more than the heads and shoulders of the bride and groom as they pass through their guard of honour under the church portico, but the three train bearers were unusual enough to warrant a special picture to themselves, for they were dressed in white Grecian tunics edged with coloured braid and had coloured shoes whose laces were cross-gartered to their knees over white stockings. The little girl's knee-length drawers show beneath her tunic; those of the boys do not. Boys were not normally train bearers in Edwardian times, and small girls usually wore dresses and hats like that of the child in picture 37. Perhaps this bride was an admirer of Isadora Duncan.

40 (below). Miss Elka Alvarez was married to Daniel Hyam at the Great Synagogue in the City of London in the summer of 1910. The wedding reception was the occasion of a great family gathering at her parents' home in Lonsdale Road, Barnes, London SW13. The bride wore a white alpaca dress and matching hat, trimmed with tulle. The bridesmaids wore pastel-coloured dresses and dark hats, lined and trimmed to match their dresses. All the hats were made by the bridegroom's mother (seated, left of the front row). Her own hat was purposely different, but she, like the bridesmaids and bride, carried a bouquet of flowers. Most of the men wore morning dress and top hats, but the two older men at the left of the picture (one of them the grandfather of the bridegroom) wore the Jewish 'kappel', the skullcap with which they normally cover their head in the synagogue. (See also picture 98.)

41 (above). *A family gathering at the wedding of Ada Gosford in 1911. Like her sister Rose (see picture 35) she married a minister of the Norbiton Primitive Methodist church and for this photograph she sat beside her husband, the Reverend William Turner, in the garden of her parents' home in Fairfield South Road, Kingston upon Thames. At this wedding none of the men wore hats although all the women and two baby nieces of the bride wore large hats. The bride wore a high-necked full-sleeved dress and a wreath and veil, but her bridesmaids, sisters of herself and her bridegroom, were dressed alike in pairs, two with the newly fashionable square yoke collar to the bodice. All four have elbow-length sleeves over high-necked, long-sleeved chemisettes.*

42 (below). *At this wedding in Walton-on-Thames only the bridesmaids wore hats for the photograph taken for the Annett family album. It was probably the summer of 1912, for the women's skirts were not as long or as full as those in previous pictures, but none of them would have been so fashion minded as to wear the new hobble skirts of high society. The bride wore a white dress, the details of which are hidden behind her bouquet, while the bridesmaids had pretty striped dresses with lace trimmings. The two older bridesmaids have tucked elbow sleeves over long lace undersleeves while the three younger girls have double puff sleeves and tucks round the bottom of their ankle-length skirts.*

These photographs also show little girls as bridesmaids, a practice which has become widespread in the twentieth century, and which has tended to replace the small boy train bearers of the late nineteenth century. Where boys are seen in Edwardian wedding photographs their fancy dress appearance is even more pronounced. The little girls were often dressed in white and their dresses were short, the normal length for a child's dress. They carried small bouquets or baskets of flowers. While most brides and bridesmaids carried flowers there are examples of photographs showing adult bridesmaids without flowers and, conversely, photographs showing the bride's mother with a floral bouquet. Flowers, lace or feathers trimmed the large hats that were always worn by bridesmaids, whether child or adult. In many Edwardian photographs the bride, bridesmaids and women guests seem to be vying with each other as to who wears the largest hat.

43. A boatman's wedding. Although in the 1890s the boatmen who worked on the inland waterways of Great Britain had been proud that their way of life was different from that of people on the land, by the time of the First World War much of that difference had disappeared. A new generation had discarded the distinctive clothes of their parents, and the young women, at least, tried to be as fashionable by general working class standards as their purse and their circumstances would allow. In this 1913 photograph, representatives of three well known boating families are pictured together at the wedding of Thirza Humphries and Herbert Baker. The bride, seated centre, wore a light-coloured dress with a cape collar, double sleeves and fashionable shoes laced across the instep. Her large hat was decorated with a big ostrich feather. Her groom wears a dark suit and a bowler hat, as does her father (in the back row), while her brother wears a large flat cap. The four children in the picture were members of the Newton family and their mother (with the baby in her lap) was the bride's sister. Their father, Charles Newton, poses in his shirtsleeves, having come straight from working a Fellows Morton and Clayton boat to the wedding reception at the Rose and Castle, Braunston, Northamptonshire, the canalside pub where many boatmen's weddings have been celebrated.

4. Wartime weddings, 1914-19

The 'golden age' of the Edwardians continued into the reign of George V with few changes in men's clothes other than the growing popularity of the lounge suit, for weddings as for other events. By 1913 and early 1914 women's skirts had become narrower and necklines occasionally lower. The S-shaped corset disappeared and the ideal fashionable woman fitted a long, narrow, draped sheath of a dress that was sometimes split up the side as far as the knee. Wedding dresses followed these lines and a soft satin material that would drape well was widely used, mainly in an ivory colour, but pale silver grey also became fashionable. Many of these dresses were embroidered in seed pearls and French knots. With the narrow, split skirt a separate tabard-like panel was added, either at the back of the waist or the shoulders, to form a train. This was also embroidered at the end with pearls to add weight and make it trail properly.

The elegant, slightly aloof image of a woman that these hobble-skirted dresses of 1912 and 1913 gave disappeared suddenly with the declaration of war in 1914. Men joined the armed forces and women took over a great deal of the men's work. Clothes became practical and the hobble skirt vanished. Hemlines rose as the war continued; they were ankle-length in 1915; 6 inches (150 mm) off the ground in 1916 and 8 inches (200 mm) off the ground in 1917.

Wedding dresses also seemed to disappear for a while. In 1915 and 1916 probably more women were married in travelling suits than in white wedding dresses. Their photographs show them wearing neat round hats, gloves, and blouses with a collar spread out over the collar and revers of the suit, which was plainly cut with a slightly flared skirt allowing easy movement. Collars were often wide – a fashion that had started on the narrower pre-war clothes – and the sailor collar became fashionable in 1917. The neck was bare and except among a few very conservative or older women the blouse came only to the collar bone.

Where a distinctive wedding dress was worn it was a slightly fuller-skirted but still floor-length adaptation of the draped and embroidered dresses of 1913, with a separate train up to 1916. After this even wedding dresses became shorter (as did evening dresses) and a typical wedding dress had a tiered full skirt and a fairly plain bodice with a vee neck filled in with a modesty vest. With these shorter dresses the veil was sometimes long enough to form the train.

beads. A Magyar-sleeved underbodice of cream ninon over lace, with a wired Medici collar and modesty vest of lace, was worn under the dress. A narrow train, edged with pearls and embroidered top and bottom with pearls and crystal beads, was fastened to the back, just below the crystal bead embroidery on the shoulders. With it, the bride wore a flower wreath and a long veil. The photograph does, however, show the bridesmaids clearly, the two older girls in fashionable softly styled two-piece suits of mid-calf length, one with a filled shawl collar, the other with a sailor collar, and the two little girls in high-waisted long-sleeved embroidered dresses, probably of organdie. All four wore wide-brimmed, fairly plain straw hats. By the time of the war light-coloured stockings were fashionable, in place of the almost universal black of Edwardian days (see picture 37), and all four of these girls wore light (probably white) stockings. The men wore dark suits and bow ties. The man on the right of the picture wore a light-coloured waistcoat. All of them wore watch chains across their waistcoats. The bridegroom was John Garnett.

47 (above). May and Ernest Baker were married at Leatherhead on 24th April 1918, and this picture shows another typical wartime wedding, with the groom and his best man both in khaki. The bride wore a mid-calf length cream satin dress with a three-layered skirt, each layer bordered with a band of gold and cream embroidery and pearls. Most of the white or cream wedding dresses from about 1912 to 1921 are lavishly decorated with pearls and cream or gold embroidery, French knots being the most popular stitch. The bodice of May's dress was square-necked (edged with pearls and embroidery) and short-sleeved. Over it she wore a waist-length sheer georgette jacket with a sailor collar and long sleeves. Her veil came down over her forehead and was held at each side by flowers. The bridesmaids had satin dresses with epaulettes on the shoulders and plain round necks. The satin of that era was difficult to press and in many photographs the deep hems of the girls' dresses show. Their hats were probably made of straw or voile on a wired frame. The bride's parents wore the fashionable clothes of 1915, or even earlier, and the bride's mother carried flowers.

Bridesmaids wore fashionable afternoon dresses, the hem well above the ankle. Their bodices had sailor collars or military epaulettes on plain round necks. Square or vee-shaped necklines were also popular; sometimes the latter had upstanding 'Medici' collars at the back. Sleeves were usually long on bridesmaids' dresses but as shorter sleeves became fashionable these too appeared towards the end of the war. The very narrow waist of the previous decade disappeared altogether and the looser fitting wartime dresses often had a rather shapeless appearance. There were many child bridesmaids and white broderie anglaise, of silk or cotton, as well as pastel coloured organdie, was used for their dresses. Stockings were now white. By the end

48. *The wedding photograph of Lieutenant Harry Hoblyn, Royal Berkshire Regiment, and Miss Gertrude Massingham, QAINS, taken at the home of the bridegroom's parents in Beckenham, Kent, after their marriage in the church of St Bartholomew the Great, Smithfield, in September 1918. The bridegroom had previously served as an NCO in the Honourable Artillery Company and was sent to the front in France in September 1914, thus becoming an 'Old Contemptible'. The couple met at the Royal Free Hospital, London, where the bride was a nursing sister, when he was invalided back to England. The bridegroom and his best man (his brother-in-law and father of the bridesmaid) both wear army uniform, as was the normal custom during the Great War for a wedding. The bride's dress is of silver-grey slipper satin, with grey silk brocade shoes; her hat is black silk with a pale pink silk lining framing her face. Her brother was unable to obtain army leave so a cousin (not able to attend the small family reception in Beckenham) gave her away. Her sister-in-law is shown in the photograph wearing a fashionable ankle-length dress. The bridegroom's father is conventionally dressed for a wedding; his mother's dress, though unfashionable in length, is black lace as she was in mourning for her son killed in action — the youngest of her nine children. She does not wear a hat because, being in poor health, she did not attend the marriage ceremony in London. The bridesmaid wears a blue silk hat, with satin ribbons and a small beading of little artificial flowers round it. Her dress is of pale blue organdie, with a tiered skirt. The photograph was taken in the conservatory at the bridegroom's parents' home. (Caption authorised by Miss Hoblyn, Mr J. G. Hoblyn and Mrs A. K. Vinicombe.)*

of the war very small girls wore white socks, showing bare knees, and these also appear on little bridesmaids. All bridesmaids wore hats, usually with moderately wide brims. Although flower-trimmed, they were not the elaborate confections of pre-war days. Little girl bridesmaids sometimes wore bonnets with very narrow brims.

Men, when not in uniform, wore similar clothes to those they had worn before the war.

49. On Monday morning 18th July 1921 Gertrude Bissett, a tailoress, married Oswald Ash at Bideford Wesleyan Methodist church. The bride wore a fashionable length saxe-blue crepe-de-chine dress with a silk facing to the kimono-sleeved bodice. The square neck had an insert of embroidery to raise it to a modest level. Her hat was of black and gold lace, trimmed only with a single gold cord and pulled well down over her eyes. The bridegroom wore a grey lounge suit and trilby hat. The wedding was reported in the local newspaper as 'A very pretty wedding' and their photograph was taken by W.H. Puddicombe of Bideford.

5. Between the wars, 1920-39

The bright young things, 1920-9

The First World War ended and Britain attempted to return to a normal peacetime existence, but the war had changed much that before had been taken for granted. Women's hemlines dropped back down to the ankle in 1919, but there was no return to the trailing skirts of Edwardian times. A new, slender line prevailed, although without the hobble effect that the couturiers had tried to introduce in the immediate pre-war days. The S-shaped corset had disappeared when the hobble skirt was fashionable, and many young women of the early 1920s did not wear corsets at all. Women had proved their abilities during the war and the ideal bride of the 1920s was a capable companion, a good sport who could help to build a new world. Fashion set out to help women give this impression.

The wedding in 1922 of King George V's daughter, Princess Mary, to Henry, Viscount Lascelles, set a precedent that was to have far reaching effects. Previous royal weddings had been, in spite of their momentary pageantry, largely for the royal family and court circles only. But as a gesture of friendliness to the women of the Empire the Queen and Princess Mary allowed details of the trousseau, the wedding dress, the presents and the future home of the couple to be published in a way that by the 1980s is taken for granted but in 1922 was new. The wedding was the grandest royal event since the coronation of the bride's father in 1911 and the newspapers reported it in great detail. For the first time since Princess Charlotte, just over one hundred years before, the bride wore silver, not white, and by so doing returned to the custom that had been followed by royalty since the middle ages.

The Times published a 'Princess Mary's Wedding' supplement on the morning of 28th February 1922 (the day of the wedding), with a sketch of the wedding dress, describing it as 'a Princess gown of cloth of silver, veiled with an overdress of ivory marquisette which is embroidered in silver and pearls. There is a full Court train of specially woven Duchess satin shot with silver. A deep border of lace cascades at the sides.' The newspaper sketches and later the photographs show a misty, fairytale gown with elbow-length sleeves and a sash formed of two ropes of pearls. It seems impossible that so fragile looking a dress could have supported the weight of the long train of heavy satin, which was embroidered with silver emblems and edged with wide

50 (above). *Princess Mary and Viscount Lascelles, with King George V and Queen Mary, after their wedding in 1922. This square-necked, narrow tunic dress with a transparent over-tunic set a pattern for wedding dresses throughout the first half of the decade. However, the majority of brides chose short rather than long wedding dresses and by holding to royal tradition the princess set herself apart from the main stream of fashion.*

51 (opposite top). *Mr and Mrs C. Willcox were married at a picturesque spring wedding at the parish church at Stonehouse, Gloucestershire. It was quite a grand affair with the groom in a dark grey morning suit and top hat, and the best man in an old fashioned frock coat and top hat, and with spats over his shoes. The very modern bride designed her own short dress and those of her bridesmaids to accentuate the season. Her dress was of white georgette, round-necked with a straight skirt, heavily tucked above the hem, over a straight white taffeta underdress; a white satin sash, tied at the front, matched the white lilies of her bouquet. The bridesmaids carried bouquets of daffodils and pussy willow and their dresses represented these two flowers. The girl on the left wore a short-sleeved yellow georgette dress with a wavy-edged three-tiered skirt over a yellow taffeta underdress, with gloves, hat and shoes to match, while the right-hand bridesmaid wore a silver grey short-sleeved georgette dress with a skirt cut in two layers of petal shapes over a silver grey taffeta underdress. She had grey shoes, gloves and hat to match. The niece of the bride, twelve years old at the time, described this wedding as 'the most beautiful thing that ever happened to her'.*

52 (right). *Albert Victor was a typical young man of the 1920s, known to his friends as a natty dresser. For his wedding to Elizabeth (known to her family as Li) in 1923 he chose a distinctive set of clothes that were of smart but sporting appearance. The trousers were of dark worsted, with turn-ups; the jacket was also dark cloth, but with the edges, pockets and cuffs bound in silk. With this suit he wore a white shirt with a wing collar, a dark tie, cream waistcoat and a cream-coloured homburg hat. His gloves were leather. Li wore a mid-calf white dress with a low round neck, plain bodice and long sleeves. The tucked skirt had an apron-like panel front and back edged with silk fringing, and an overskirt of exceptionally fine georgette, made in two pieces meeting front and back and veiling the apron panels. Her large bouquet was of white chrysanthemums.*

53. *Dorothy Bennett and Sidney Ball were married at St Stephen's church, East Putney, London, at the end of October 1925 (left). Dorothy's very elegant dress, edged with a chiffon neck frill, was of cream satin, straight-cut with no waistline and a pleated skirt set very low down at centre front and back, rising to hip level at the sides. The pearl trimming to the top edge of the skirt was taken from another dress and she borrowed a lace handkerchief and wore blue garters under her dress to hold up her white stockings. Dorothy had two child bridesmaids dressed in pale blue silk with blue lace bonnets, and her youngest brother as a page boy in a sapphire blue velvet suit with a lace collar and dark pumps with straps crossing on the instep (right).*

Honiton lace. The dress itself is now kept at the Bethnal Green Museum and belies its appearance, for it is extraordinarily heavy to handle. The underdress is made of silver lamé, covered with a tunic of fine net heavily embroidered in a trellis design of roses made of seed pearls and crystals. The train is held to the shoulders by two clasps covered by further pearl and crystal embroidery.

Trains were fashionable with royal and society brides. Lady Elizabeth Bowes-Lyon, bride of the Duke of York (later George VI), had a separate train fastened to the hips of her narrow ivory

54. *In Scotland the law provides for a clergyman to conduct a wedding ceremony in places other than a church. Weddings, therefore, have frequently been held in private houses or in the room where the wedding reception was to take place. Burlington House, in Bath Street, Glasgow, was a suite of reception rooms, used for various kinds of functions, especially weddings. In 1928 Andrew Borland and Elizabeth Young were married there and were photographed on the imposing steps of the main entrance. Both of them were over forty when they were married and their wedding was quietly formal and dignified. The bride wore a low-waisted long-sleeved dress of chiffon and lace with white stockings and a lace cloche hat. Her bouquet, although fashionably large with roses set among trailing fern, gave as delicate an impression as her dress. The bridegroom wore a morning suit over a white shirt and wing collar, completing his outfit with a pale grey tie. Over the lacing of his shoes he wore a pair of pale grey spats, their straps passing below the insteps to keep them in place. These were a fashionable part of formal dress among the middle class until the late 1930s. As Mr Borland was an agent for the Irvine Valley Lace Mills, his bride's dress and hat were an appropriate complement to him.*

55 (above). *This photograph in the Merseyside County Museum shows the wedding group of William Johnson and his bride, Emily Leigh, at Macclesfield in 1928. The picture was taken in the backyard of the bride's parents' home and shows the bridegroom in his best suit, formalised for the occasion by a wing collar. The bride wore a simple short white dress with a vee neck; her full veil was held down to her forehead by a wreath of orange blossom. The three adult bridesmaids wore short, light-coloured dresses, with big collars and cloche hats. The child bridesmaid, youngest sister of the bride, also wore a cloche hat above a low-waisted dress with a short skirt composed entirely of rows of frills. This style is the forerunner of all the little girls' dresses of the 1930s with their frilled skirts. The little page-boy wore shorts and a white shirt.*

56 (left). *While most wedding dresses of the 1920s were short, not all were white, and many girls were married in their best shift dress and a cloche hat. This picture shows the bride and groom, Olwen and Llew, looking little different from the bridesmaid and best man. The photograph was taken in 1929 at Cynwyd, near Corwen, North Wales.*

57. *A very fashion-conscious bride posed in a garden at Highbury, London, with her husband, best man and bridesmaids. The two men wore lounge suits, the groom having a wing collar to his shirt and white spats over his shoes. The bride and her bridesmaids wore the tiered skirts with hemlines higher at the front than the back that were high fashion in the summer of 1929. The bridesmaids' dresses were sleeveless, with low round necklines; they wore bands of ribbon across their hair with a small posy of flowers over each ear. The little girl bridesmaid wore a square-necked dress with an uneven waistline, high at the front, low at the back, and a two-tiered scalloped skirt edged with small frills. Her head-dress matched those of the other bridesmaids. The bride wore a most unusual pointed pixie-like bonnet that seems to be composed entirely of flower buds. Her long veil hung from the back of this cap and would have trailed on the floor had her little bridesmaid not carried it.*

and silver wedding dress in 1923. She also had a second train of tulle from the shoulders, above which floated her veil, held down to her forehead by a narrow band covered with myrtle leaves, ending in two white roses and orange blossom over each ear. She was the last royal bride to wear flowers in her hair. Her dress was lighter in weight than Princess Mary's, but both were long, not quite touching the floor. Lady Elizabeth had been a bridesmaid to Princess Mary, and at both these weddings the bridesmaids had worn white and silver dresses with skirts reaching to just above the ankle.

Most brides of the 1920s followed the fashion set by the royal bridesmaids rather than the royal brides. Wedding dresses were made in the fashionable afternoon dress length that shrank steadily throughout the decade until 1929, when the back of the skirt, though not the front, dropped dramatically. In 1921 and 1922 the hemline varied between just above the ankle and mid calf. Many wedding photographs show brides and bridesmaids wearing this length of skirt, while older women guests still wear ankle-length or even floor-length dresses. There were few differences in young women's clothes to denote class. Correct formal wear for men in this period was the morning coat, either black or grey, although some older men occasionally wore pre-war frock coats. Black or grey top hats could be worn. Middle-class and working men wore lounge suits, usually dark (black or blue), and carried trilby hats, the new smart wear of the ex-serviceman, while straw boaters were occasionally still seen at summer weddings.

Although cream silk and soft satin were popular, 1920s wedding dresses were not always cream or white. Pastel colours were fashionable for afternoon dresses and many dresses were made by the brides themselves to be worn for best afterwards. Blue was popular, from the old rhyme 'Married in blue, you will always be true', and the colour and fabrics could range from the palest forget-me-not blue silk to deep blue velvet. Pale blush pink or peach were other popular colours, especially in the second half of the decade when wedding dresses again began to resemble evening dresses rather than day dresses. Some elaborately beaded and embroidered examples survive in museum collections. Sometimes the beaded trimmings were taken from former dresses and reused, perhaps by a sister or cousin for her own wedding dress. There were no rules about hats or veils for brides; a hat could be worn with a white dress or a veil with a coloured one. Many veils were worn by more than one bride, being loaned in turn to all the sisters in a family. Even royalty did this, for Lady Elizabeth Bowes-Lyon's veil was loaned to her by her mother-in-law, Queen Mary. When a veil was worn it was invariably clamped low down on the forehead.

Bridesmaids wore stylish day dresses and many 1920s photographs can be accurately dated by the bridesmaids' dresses, both in style and length. Apron-like tunics, tabards and overskirts were worn from 1922 to 1924; the waistline became non-existent in 1925, to reappear low down on the hips, often with gathers or shirring at this line, in 1926-7. Scalloped, petal-edged skirts were popular in 1927, asymmetrical trimmings or drapings in 1928. The back of the skirt became longer than the front in 1929, to be followed by longer, even-all-round skirts in 1930. The cloche hat,

58. *Skirts become longer in 1930, and the decade of short wedding dresses was over. This unknown bride of the early 1930s wore a floor-length, long-sleeved dress with a U-shaped neckline, probably with a lace modesty piece tucked inside it (hidden in this picture by her bouquet), a two-stranded pearl necklace and a large deep-crowned lacy hat rather like a very wide-brimmed cloche. Her bridegroom wore a lounge suit of rather old-fashioned cut (about 1925) and carried a bowler hat.*

pulled well down over the eyebrows, covering the forehead, was almost universally worn from 1925 to 1929. Many bridesmaids wore cloche hats, trimmed or untrimmed, in materials ranging from the same fabric as their dresses to straws of various colours.

Little girl bridesmaids wore tucked or tiered dresses, falling from high yokes at the beginning of the decade, or from a low waistline in 1927 and 1928, or from shaped waistbands, high in the front and low at the back, in 1929. 'Dutch' style bonnets, with little wings at the sides, were the most favoured style of head-dresses for these little girls, all through the decade. Small boys were still popular as pages and were usually dressed in velvet or satin 'buster suits'. Both boys and girls wore knee-length white socks.

59. *Mr and Mrs Rogers were married in London in 1932. The bride wore a medieval-type long-sleeved ankle-length dress of white crepe, with a deep vee neck. Her long embroidered veil was attached to the back of a white lace Dutch-style bonnet and formed a drifting gauzy train. The white flowers carried by the bride were tied with a white satin bow and were set off with a long trail of greenery. The bridegroom wore a grey suit with a stylish double-breasted waistcoat. His homburg hat and gloves were pale grey.*

60. *Women's wedding fashions became distinctly medieval in style during the first years of the 1930s. White chiffon velvet for brides' dresses was matched by vividly coloured chiffon velvet bridesmaids' dresses, like Hollywood versions of fourteenth-century court ladies. Typical were these two girls in 1931, the older girl in a long crimson velvet dress with a square neckline, low waist and long, tight sleeves. The younger girl wore pale green velvet with a round neck and short sleeves. Her skirt was mid-calf length. They both wore imitation tiaras and carried bouquets of tulips and daffodils.*

The Hollywood influence, 1930-9

The period from 1930 to 1939 was the decade in which the 'bright young things' of the 1920s passed into maturity, while their younger successors were influenced by the cinema. Day dress lengths were longer but their styles were plainer, and because of mass production there was little class distinction in women's day clothes. Evening dresses were of varied designs, from the sophisticated, slim-fitting, backless sheath to the demure, puffed sleeved, gathered skirted 'mock Victorian' dresses considered suitable evening wear for young women. Wedding dresses turned to romantic styles, influenced by the historical epics of the cinema, or to the plainer evening dress styles where the intricacy of their cut (often a complicated bias cut) achieved a simplicity of effect that was almost impossible to mass-produce or make cheaply. The supreme representative of this type of dress was that of Princess Marina, who in 1934 married the Duke of Kent wearing a long, slim, silver lamé dress with a cowl neckline and wide, graceful sleeves. The dress had a

61 (above). *This 1934 bride chose a flowered 'garden-party' long-skirted summer two-piece for her wedding. By the mid 1930s women's clothes had begun to develop padded shoulders and this suit had such fashionable shoulders. Her hat was very up-to-date, shallow-crowned, wide-brimmed, and worn dipping to one side. Her groom wore a light-coloured summer lounge suit, and her two bridesmaids wore short-sleeved dresses with skirts composed of rows of little frills.*

62 (left). *Frills were popular decorations for children's party dresses and bridesmaids' dresses in the 1930s (see also pictures 5 and 61). This little girl was a very proud bridesmaid at a Welsh wedding in 1934. Her short-sleeved long dress was trimmed with lace and had a cape collar and a double row of frills at the hem. The wreath of rosebuds on her hair echoed the flower pattern of her dress. She carried a tall basket of flowers and fern.*

long court train from the shoulders and her long tulle veil was held on the top of her head by a tiara with upstanding points like the rays of the sun. Although the dress was impossible to copy, many brides of the later 1930s wore a 'Princess Marina' head-dress made in glass, paste or fake pearls.

But with the vogue for romance in the early 1930s even day dresses could be floor-length and many summer brides were married in long 'garden party' dresses of flowered chiffon, or of silk or lace. These dresses always had long sleeves, or a long-sleeved jacket was worn over a matching sleeveless dress. With these dresses they wore straw hats, often trimmed with a simple ribbon. The hats were shallow-crowned, sometimes with wide brims that dipped in the front – the 'Dolly Varden' picture hat — or they were small brimmed cloches, no longer pulled down over the eyebrows but perched up on top of the head. Veils do not seem to have been worn with these coloured day dresses. Pearl necklaces were favourite wear for brides, whether in white or coloured dresses, and are often quoted in newspaper reports as being 'the gift of the bridegroom'. From 1937, the heart-shaped or 'sweetheart' neckline appeared, a fashion that was to continue in favour for ten or more years. Shoulders even in wedding dresses became padded, and the long sleeves were gathered at the

63. *Wedding dresses and bridesmaids' dresses became plainer and simpler in cut as the 1930s progressed, although the fabric from which they were made became more distinctive. Mary Blakeley was married at Church Fenton Methodist church three years after her sister Marjorie (see picture 5), but instead of lace and flowers Mary wore bridal satin and a 'Princess Marina' diadem-shaped tiara for her wedding in September 1936 to Edgar Beverley. Her bridesmaids wore long dresses with padded shoulders and wide collars, short puffed sleeves and long above-the-elbow gloves. They also wore Juliet caps edged with lace.*

64. *This photograph, now in Carlisle Museum, shows the typical 'jewelled' simplicity of late 1930s wedding dresses. The dress is also part of the museum collection and is made of ivory satin with five fleur-de-lis motives of pearl and gilt glass beads sewn to the centre front of the dress. The head-dress consists of three fleur-de-lis of pearls and gilt, glued on to a stiff back and mounted on a satin band. The dress has a sweetheart neckline edged with a narrow frill of pleated satin; the shoulders are padded, and the sleeves are long and narrow. The skirt starts just below the bust and sweeps out into a long train, which has another fleur-de-lis jewelled motif near its hem.*

shoulder and cut in a vee shape to lie over the back of the hand. The white wedding became firmly established as a tradition in the late 1930s and a colder white satin became popular, gradually ousting the ivory and cream fabrics that had been worn as 'white' for nearly half a century. This satin was sometimes woven in a damask-like flower pattern that eventually became known as 'bridal satin'. White wedding dresses became 'special', not meant to be worn at any other function.

65. *A village wedding in Cornwall in 1938, when the churchwarden of Flushing, Miss May Olivey, married Bernard Heale, an agricultural scientist. They were both pillars of local society and their wedding was a grand occasion by village standards. The bride considered she was too mature for a white dress and chose to wear a garden-party dress with a diagonally pleated yoke, padded shoulders and short puffed sleeves. With this dress she wore mittens and a hat completely covered in flowers, to match her large bouquet, which was surrounded by a white paper lace frill. Her bridegroom wore a light grey lounge suit and no hat.*

For men the formal morning coat, grey striped trousers and pale grey waistcoats continued as a wedding uniform. Grey top hats gradually replaced black ones. Wing collars and spats, both worn in the 1920s, had disappeared by the end of the decade. But the formal suit, now often hired for the occasion, was slowly giving way to the dark lounge suit as accepted wear to accompany brides in white. A 'fifty shilling suit' (a characteristic of the 1930s) was often a young man's first complete suit of clothes and many of them, worn only for best, lasted well into the 1950s, sometimes accompanying a daughter to her own wedding. Where informal weddings took place, with brides in coloured dresses, men wore lighter clothes, grey or brown being favoured. No hats were worn by the men in lounge suits, but a white flower was worn in the buttonhole and a white handkerchief was thrust into the breast pocket.

Bridesmaids' dresses were also romantic in the 1930s and became influenced by film or evening dress styles rather than by day dresses. They were often long dresses in vivid colours that were never quite right for any other occasion. In an attempt to make them more useful they were sometimes sleeveless, or even backless, but were worn with matching elbow-length capes and long gloves. By the end of the decade they were usually short-sleeved and long gloves matching the colour of the dress were almost universal. However, even the short-sleeved dresses never looked right as evening dresses, and like the bride's dress they became a recognisable garment that had little relationship to any other function.

Dresses for small girl bridesmaids usually had frilled skirts. When short, as the younger girls' dresses usually were, they could be worn again as party dresses, but many of the ankle-length bridesmaids' dresses worn by girls of nine to thirteen years of age were relegated to the family dressing-up box to appear again as stage costumes or be worn by attendants to the school or village May Queen. Small boys appear to have become much more self-conscious in the 1930s and fewer of them appear as attendants in wedding photographs.

6. Austerity and after, 1940-52

Far more than during the First World War fashion came to a standstill during the years 1940 to 1945. Clothes rationing was introduced in 1941 and continued for the next nine to ten years. For two years the fashions set in 1939 held sway, then in 1942 'utility' clothes were introduced. Standard designs for nearly all garments were produced by a committee; it aimed at achieving the maximum use of the minimum of cloth and all unessential decoration was banished. But the utility scheme did set a minimum standard below which design and production should not fall and it was a reasonable one, if rather monotonous.

In spite of the war and the almost uniform-like sameness of civilian clothing (or perhaps because of it) many women still wanted a white wedding that would remain a bright memory in a time of hardship. Wedding dresses from the 1930s were loaned to younger sisters, or new ones were contrived by families contributing clothing coupons. Almost invariably the skirts of these white wedding dresses were long, if rather narrow. Necklines were high and round, or square or heart-shaped. Sleeves were long and tight. The dress and fabrics were rather plain. Day dresses often had small shoulder yokes and pads: so did many wedding dresses. Veils were often borrowed and these were long 1930s veils. New veils were often only shoulder length.

At the start of the war there were still many formal weddings with men in morning suits and small bridesmaids in pastel-coloured, long-skirted, short-sleeved voile dresses, but as more and more men joined the services their uniform became the accepted formal men's wear for weddings and the morning suit seemed out of place. As the war went on many women entered the services and met and married fellow servicemen, both bride and groom wearing their uniforms for the ceremony. Many civilian brides did not have a white wedding, and for these girls a neat 'utility' suit with a straight skirt (two inverted pleats in front and one at the back) and a semi-fitted jacket with padded shoulders was the most popular wear. It was brightened by a small hat, perched well forward on the head or tilted over one eye, with a little veil, and a spray of flowers pinned to the lapel of the suit. Little gloves crocheted from white cotton were often worn as well. There were usually no bridesmaids at these wartime weddings, although the bride and groom would be supported by their colleagues, fellow officers or servicemen, and many of them

66. *At first the Second World War made little difference in weddings. On 31st August 1940 Susanne Mills was married to Maurice Keating at St John the Baptist church, Cookham Dean, Berkshire. It could have been any time in the late 1930s, with the groom in morning clothes, the bride in a turtle-necked close-fitting long-sleeved wedding dress with a court train hung from the shoulders and carried by a small page in white satin shirt and grey shorts. The two little bridesmaids wore tulle dresses with frilled, short-sleeved bodices. Their head-dresses and that of the bride were of mother-of-pearl and gilt.*

walked under archways of swords, truncheons and even air-raid wardens' hats after the ceremony.

In 1945, when men began to be discharged from the services and there was a spate of weddings, white wedding dresses were still the plain slender sheaths they had been in 1941, but the skirt was trained slightly, a fashion that had gone out in the war years. The train was to grow longer and longer until the 1950s, when it began to disappear again. Fashion, newly released by the end of the war, plunged into the 'New Look' of nipped-in waist, closely fitted bodice, padded hips and a longer daytime skirt. Although clothes were still rationed, women wanted to be fashionable and many went to a great deal of trouble to achieve this. Home dressmaking became very popular as buying the material to make up was more economical, in money and coupons, than buying a garment ready made. For brides with few coupons a new New

67 (right). *By 1941 the effect of the war was beginning to show and grand 'white' weddings became the exception rather than the rule. This contemporary photograph shows Nina and George Tinns, after their wedding on 3rd April 1941, passing under an arch made of air-raid wardens' tin hats, held by their fellow wardens. (Both Nina and George were air-raid wardens at the time.) Both of them wore navy-blue pin-stripe suits; Nina had a box-pleated skirt. Her hat was a flowered and veiled pillbox, worn jauntily at one side. Note the gasmask carried, even to a wedding, by the warden on the right.*

68 (below). *At the wedding of Third Officer Joan Rouff of the WRNS and Lieutenant D. Campbell of the RNR the bride's fellow officers provided the guard of honour for the newly married couple, both in uniform. They were married at St Patrick's church, Greenock, in January 1942.*

69 (above). *A picture officially released by the War Office in 1943 with the heading 'Wing Commander Jameson's wedding, at a country church, somewhere in England'. The accompanying text read 'Wing Commander Patrick G. Jameson, DFC, twentynine year old native of Wellington, New Zealand, was married recently to Miss Hilda Webster, also of Wellington, New Zealand, who arrived in England for the wedding a few days previously. Wing Commander Jameson frequently leads a Spitfire wing in sweeps over occupied territory and won his DFC for gallantry in the Narvik Sea when he set on fire two four-engined flying boats hidden in a fiord.' The picture shows Mr and Mrs Jameson after the wedding watching a fly-past of his squadron over the church. The bride wears a classic 1930s type white silk dress and a veil.*

70 (left). *Immediately post-war, Desmond Motley wears a 'demob' style suit for his wedding. His bride, Elsie, wears a dress with padded shoulders and a stand-up collar echoing the styles of the late 1930s. However, the skirt drapery, caught up to reveal the frilled petticoat, is very much a post-war feature.*

71 (right). *An advertisement from the 'New English Review', November 1946. Note the emphasis on saving clothing coupons. The picture shows the 'uniform' morning suit of striped trousers, grey waistcoat and black cut-away jacket, considered the correct formal wear for men at weddings at this time.*

72 (below). *At Brenda and Douglas Ashford's wedding at St John's church, Hampton Wick, Middlesex, in 1947 all the men hired morning suits for the occasion. The bride and her four bridesmaids, however, gave up clothing coupons for their dresses. These all had padded shoulders and sweetheart necklines. The bride's white satin dress had a short train. The bridesmaids' dresses, although pretty, were neither fashionable day nor evening wear; the girl on the right kept her pink grosgrain silk dress and cut it to mid-calf length when the New Look became fashionable in 1949.*

73 (above). *Corporal Jack Bernard Kitson (Signals) and Eliza Womersley, known to her friends and relations as Bette, were married on 2nd April 1949 at St Mary's parish church, Illingworth, Halifax, West Yorkshire. The bride's outfit was a dress and jacket in dusky pink crepe with burgundy velvet 'love-knot' trimming. It was a 'Model' made by Elsie Whitely of Halifax and cost 4 guineas. The close-fitting hat, of burgundy feathers with a burgundy veil, was specially made by Shaw Hardcastle Ltd of Halifax, who sent it to London to be trimmed. It was trimmed free as it was for a wedding and cost 19s 11d including postage. The shoes were burgundy suede court shoes and cost 9s 11d. Her gloves were also burgundy colour and cost 1s 11d. The groom wore his uniform. Their respective mothers wore their best clothes made to the typical 'utility' designs that characterised the 1940s.*

74 (opposite). *Not until the end of the 1940s could the creators of wedding dresses exercise their full talents. Mrs E. Wadsworth (who had trained at the dressmakers Frisby Dyke of Liverpool and later set up her own business in Crosby, where she dressed two generations of the leading families) was by that time elderly and in failing health. Nevertheless she made this superb dress for Miss Nora Davies as a final masterpiece. It was of soft silk satin with a crepe weave, plainly cut, with sleeves that were long, pointed at the wrist, and slightly gathered to padded shoulders. The bodice fastened at the back with small self-covered buttons, while the long gored skirt swept out into a great train. A separate basque was attached to the belt at the back and was trimmed with small rouleau bows of the dress fabric. The veil and head-dress were made by another famous Liverpool firm, Cripps, the head-dress incorporating a sentimental mixture of orange blossom (made of white kid) from the bride's grandmother's wedding wreath and flowers from her mother's wedding head-dress. The bouquet was all white and included gardenias, stephanotis, camellias and white heather. Miss Davies, a former subaltern in the ATS, married the Reverend H. Whilton at St Luke's church, Great Crosby, in August 1949. Her dress and photograph are now in the Merseyside County Museums collection. The photograph is by E. Chambre-Hardman FRPS of Liverpool.*

75. For her wedding to Eric Rooke on 8th March 1950 at the registry office in Wandsworth Town Hall, Valerie Diggins chose to wear a New Look suit and matching coat in a light grey worsted fabric that she had bought, and surrendered clothing coupons for, the year before. With these she wore a powder-blue blouse and navy blue platform-soled wedge-heeled shoes for which she gave up seven coupons. Accessories were in short supply but she managed to find a matching navy blue velvet hat with a pale blue feather and leather gloves; after queuing for an hour at a London store she added a navy blue leather handbag to her outfit. Eric wore a new, non-utility suit made in the new 'American' double-breasted style with long lapels, which had a buttonhole worked in the top of each (a feature which had completely disappeared from English utility suits).

Look suit with its ultra-feminine contours made a becoming wedding outfit, especially if worn with a small, veiled, flower-covered pillbox hat in summer, or given fur cuffs and a fur pillbox hat for winter. Many girls made their own white wedding dresses, or their mothers made them, and the bridal section in the pattern catalogues grew larger. Patterns designed for wedding and bridesmaids' dresses had been available from the end of the First World War, but only during and after the Second World War did home dressmaking become universally accepted among all social classes.

In 1945 some fabrics were free of coupons, notably former Royal Air Force parachutes. Offered for sale whole or in 11 foot (3.35 m) triangular panels they were a godsend to the home

76. *The Reverend George D. Wilkie and Marguerite (Rita) Sutherland were married in Laurieknowe church, Dumfries, in April 1951. Although he was an ordained minister, at St Martin's Church of Scotland, Port Glasgow, George Wilkie considered a sombre clerical outfit, which was his normal daily wear, to be inappropriate for his wedding. He therefore borrowed a kilt of his own family tartan to make the occasion a truly colourful Scottish event. His best man, William Stirling, also wore a kilt. Rita wore a fitted dress of white broché slipper satin with a sweetheart neckline and long sleeves. Her veil was of tulle worn with a pearl head-dress and her bouquet was of crimson carnations, lily of the valley and freesia. The two bridesmaids wore tulle dresses over taffeta underdresses, one in lilac with a bouquet of mauve tulips and freesia, the other in sea-green with a bouquet of pink tulips. The two young train bearers wore short dresses of embroidered white organdie with pink sashes.*

dressmaker; some were made of the new synthetic nylon and were usually white or lime green, although orange-coloured ones could occasionally be obtained. While few wedding dresses were made from parachutes, because the fabric was slippery to handle, difficult to sew and did not always hang well when finished, many a bridal petticoat and honeymoon nightdress was made from it, and at least one fair-haired little girl bridesmaid wore a dress made from a lime green parachute panel. Trimmed with some pre-war lace, it looked very pretty.

Many a groom and his 'best man' had hired their morning suits in pre-war days, and this practice continued after the war, but the hiring of dresses for brides and bridesmaids only began after the war. However, for the cost of a dress which might only be worn once, a bride could hire an outfit which would originally cost some four or five times as much and which would, therefore, have been correspondingly more elegant. Also it would not have used up any precious clothing coupons.

The demobilisation of the forces was spread out over a further two years after the war. In addition, national service was introduced for all young men between eighteen and twenty. This was deferred until after graduation for university students. As a consequence many bridegrooms immediately after the war wore their uniforms at their weddings. Many wore buttonholes of carnations with these uniforms although this was officially frowned upon in service regulations. Only the Royal Navy had a tradition of a wedding uniform – when an able seaman marries he ties his scarf with white ribbons so that he wears a satin bow and streamers on his chest – and many a young naval rating followed this tradition. Other post-war grooms wore their 'demob' suit with which all newly released servicemen were issued for civilian life.

Post-war bridesmaids' dresses were usually long-skirted versions of the currently fashionable day dresses in various flower colours. These dresses were sometimes worn as dance dresses afterwards, although they were somehow never sufficiently dramatic or fashionable. Sometimes girls cut them short to the mid-calf ballerina length, when they became more satisfactory best or party dresses. By the early 1950s, when clothes rationing had ceased, many bridesmaids' dresses were made mid-calf length to start with and were modelled on the fashionable short evening or cocktail dress. Little girls also wore short dresses, but there are few examples of small boys as attendants in the immediate post-war years.

7. The second Elizabethans, 1953-80

A time of optimism, 1953-69

Queen Elizabeth II was crowned in Westminster Abbey in June 1953. Six years earlier, when she was Princess Elizabeth, her wedding, also at Westminster Abbey, had been an 'austerity' wedding. In spite of the magnificent embroidery on her gown, its basic design of fitted bodice, sweetheart neckline, padded shoulders, long sleeves and long slightly gathered skirt had been worn by many late 1940s brides, and like them she had to give up clothing coupons for it. Unlike other girls, the princess had been granted a special allowance of clothing coupons; the wedding was seen as a boost for national morale and prestige, and her dress had a separate train that stretched 14 yards (12.8 m) behind her. All this additional fabric took the extra coupons. The lavish embroidery on the dress was repeated on the skirts of the bridesmaids' dresses; they had also been granted a special allowance of clothing coupons. But by 1953 clothing coupons had been abolished and there was a new optimistic outlook for fashion, as for everything else.

The 1950s and 1960s were decades of growth and expansion. The consumer society was born, and fashions became shorter lived, a parallel to the 1920s when designs changed year by year. Although most women do not throw away all their clothes and buy new each year, wedding dresses are usually as up-to-date as possible. The extravagances of the late 1940s New Look had been modified to a more natural though still elegant line. Waists were small, skirts were full and of mid-calf length. The alternative, a narrow skirt, still of mid-calf length and slit at the bottom, was equally popular, and although it does not seem to have influenced white wedding dresses, it was worn as a suit style to many registry office weddings.

The 1950s fashion designers produced a bewildering number of variations in the basic line of dresses, including the 'A line' (widening to the hem with a low belt, or gathering at the hips), the 'Y line' (an inverted Y shape, achieved with the help of flying panels, flowing skirts and capes), the 'H line' (straight, but with a band or swathing at the hips) and finally the 'sack line' (a dress or coat that hung straight from the shoulders without a belt). Common to all these lines before the 'sack' was the wealth of detail in cutting and seaming to give the basic shape to the dress. The square neck and the sweetheart neck disappeared: fancy-

77. Elaborate cakes for wedding receptions have always been popular. Two-tier cakes were fashionable in the 1950s, as were photographs showing the bride and groom cutting their cake. This picture shows John Forde and his bride, Euphrasie, at the reception after their wedding at St Margaret's church, Putney, SW15, on 16th May 1953. He wore a double-breasted dark-grey lounge suit with turn-ups, a white shirt and a grey silk tie. She wore a circular-skirted, ballerina-length, halter-necked dress of white tulle over taffeta. The bodice was edged with heavy guipure lace, which formed the halter strap and also a belt around the waist. Over the halter-necked dress she wore a long-sleeved, unlined, tulle bolero with a small mandarin collar edged with lace. Her waist-length veil was held by a Juliet cap covered with lace and embroidered with pearls.

shaped yokes to dresses were quite common and wedding dresses could have plain round or slightly vee-shaped necklines following the line of the yoke. Without yokes they had boat-shaped necklines or even the wide vee-shaped, almost off the shoulder neckline with a stand-up draped shawl collar that became the hallmark of the mid 1950s fashions.

Romantic white wedding dresses in the 1950s tended to be conservative in design, following the basic pattern of fitted bodice, long sleeves and long skirts. The details place them firmly in their own decade – sloping shoulders, narrower waists, wider skirts and diminishing trains – as does the fabric, for patterns were bold and popular even in white bridal brocades and satins unsullied by any other colour. The short evening dress became both fashionable and popular in the 1950s and with it the short white wedding dress, another parallel to the 1920s. But the short wedding dresses of the 1950s were quite distinct from those of the 1920s, being much more shapely, worn over short wide petticoats, with short or waist-length circular veils held well off the wearer's face.

Fashionable bridesmaids wore short dresses; this was common even when the bride wore a long dress. These bridesmaids' dresses were usually short-sleeved and worn with matching gloves. Two bridesmaids were the popular number, and they followed the A line, the Y line or even wilder extravagances of fashion, the puffball or barrel line (a full skirt gathered at the top to the fitted bodice of the dress, and at the bottom to a band that was much narrower than the skirt itself). With these well cut and structured dresses, hats were fashionable, notably the pillbox, made in a matching fabric. Another widely worn fashion of the 1950s was the 'half-hat', a 3-4 inch (75-100 mm) wide shaped band of buckram wired round the edges to grip the head and covered

78. *When Doris Wells married Leon Bass at Bunyan Baptist church, Kingston upon Thames, in 1954 she wanted a grand traditional wedding dress rather than a fashionable short one. A friend designed and made for her this wide-skirted, corselet-waisted white silk brocade dress with its unusual heart-shaped yoke. All the seams in the dress were piped with plain white silk over a white cord. The dress had a very slight train.*

82. *Captain Ralph May of the Border Regiment, Carlisle, was a widower with a small son when he married Bridget, the daughter of Colonel Rutherford, in 1957. It was intended to be a quiet wedding but turned into a very happy full-scale military family occasion. Captain May, his fellow officers and NCOs (who formed the guard of honour) wore 'number one dress' or 'blue patrols'. His son wore a miniature copy of the full dress uniform of the Border Regiment. Bridget was a nurse at the King Edward VII Hospital for Officers and she bought heavy satin from a furnishing shop in London for her dress, which was made by Miss Porterhouse, a Carlisle dressmaker. The dress had a boat-shaped neckline with a rolled collar, tight-fitting sleeves and a wide pleated band from waist to hip which became a draped bustle-like sash at the back, trailing slightly at the hem to make a short train. She had a short circular silk veil and carried pale pink roses. Her bridesmaids wore short white crystal organza dresses with full skirts. They wore circlets of rose hips, corn and yellow and white freesias and carried posies of the same flowers. The photograph was taken by the 'Cumberland News', Carlisle.*

a white wedding dress, and in the late 1950s narrow 'peg-top' skirted dresses with matching very short jackets appeared; with these were worn 'Breton' type sailor hats, with upturned brims. A large flower in the hat and at the neck of the jacket transformed these outfits into wedding garments.

Although Mary Quant introduced the first just above the knee mini-dresses in 1958, it was not until the mid 1960s that skirts rose to knee high, and then above, for all women. New synthetic fabrics were introduced, notably crimplene, a textured, machine-knitted material that was ideally suited to the simple basic shapes of the 1960s dresses.

By the late 1960s the conservatism shown in wedding dresses since the end of the war was disappearing and an element of fancy dress was beginning to creep in. Brides' and bridesmaids' dresses were copied from all historical periods. This was not altogether new. Although Princess Mary's dress in 1922 had been modern for its time, her sister-in-law, the Lady Elizabeth Bowes-Lyon,

83 (above). *In 1961 Christine Gumbrell was the 'Brown Owl' of the 6th Kingston upon Thames Brownie pack. When she married Anthony Gibb at the Eden Street Methodist church the Brownies formed a guard of honour as they left the church after the service.*
84 (right). *When Mr and Mrs R. White were married at the church of St Philip and St James in the village of Burtle, Somerset, the local children perpetuated the traditional village custom of tying the gates of the churchyard shut with string and wire. Every best man at the weddings in this church must make sure that he has a pocket knife and wire cutters with him. Other people at the wedding throw handfuls of coins over the gate to the children.*

85. *The millionaire's daughter Teleri Hughes wore a white silk and lace wedding dress designed by French couturier Jacques Heim for her wedding to the banker Cyril Jones on 23rd September 1961. The dress had three-quarter sleeves and a rounded neckline and, although described by the 'Liverpool Daily Post' as 'a medieval styled wedding gown' it was very much in keeping with high fashion of the early 1960s. The details which raised it above what most brides of the time could afford were the panels of hand embroidery on the lace to accentuate the design and the separate train which was lined with a delicate pink silk. An outstanding head-dress, consisting of a circlet of orange blossom with a rose at each side, perched on the top of her head securing a fold of her long silk veil, but even this effect was fashionable among other brides of the time, although most of them settled for a single large rose on the top of the head (see picture 86). The rare old Welsh harp, beside which the bride posed for this photograph, was played at the wedding reception by Telynores Maldwyn, the noted Welsh harpist. The last time this harp had been played at a wedding was over a hundred years before. Photograph by E. Chambre-Hardman.*

86. *Tangerine and apricot were popular colours for bridesmaids' dresses in the early 1960s. These three girls wore simple short dresses of apricot crimplene, the two older girls with crossover skirts, the little girl with a square yoke forming tiny cap sleeves. All three wore short white nylon gloves and white shoes. The bride, Brenda, married to William Hern at Dartford, Kent, in 1962, wore a very plain dress of white satin. Her veil was held in place by a single white rose on the top of her head. This was a very fashionable innovation of the early 1960s and milliners and fashion writers nicknamed it a 'miner's lamp'.*

87 (above). *This formal wedding at Norton St Philip, near Bath, was reported in the 'Bath and Wilts Evening Chronicle' under the headline 'Personalities of theatre married'. The bride was Anthea Olive, the designer and wardrobe mistress of the Liverpool Everyman Theatre Company. The bridegroom was Peter James, a director of the company. Peter James and his best man, Christopher Bradley, wore black morning suits with grey top hats. His bride wore a cream ribbed-silk dress designed by herself to complement the Honiton lace veil, an heirloom which had been worn by generations of brides. Anthea's sister, Maria, wore a short dress of cream linen embroidered with white daisies and white stockings, a very fashionable mid 1960s detail, as were the real white Shaster daisies worn as crowns on their heads and carried as tight posies by both girls.*

88 (left). *Little bridesmaids wore short dresses in the 1960s. These two, aged nine and seven years, were bridesmaids on a cold February day at Worthing in 1965. They wore dresses and jackets of corn-coloured fine corduroy velvet. The fronts of the short-sleeved dresses were covered with rows of nylon lace. The silk-lined jackets had a single fastening at the neck, so that the lace showed beneath them. Their Juliet caps were petal-shaped.*

89. *In 1967 Lieutenants Sylvia Gore and Peter Dalziel, two members of the Salvation Army 'Joystrings' musical group, were married at the Addington Citadel, near Croydon, Surrey. Although they were in uniform it was a departure from the traditional Salvation Army wedding for Sylvia carried a bouquet of flowers and did not wear the heavy white silk bridal cord or scarf which until the 1950s it had been customary for female Salvation Army officers to wear, draped from left shoulder to right hip, at their weddings. In a Salvation Army officers' uniformed wedding the young couple stand on the platform before the Salvation Army flag, facing the congregation, to make their vows. The officiating officer stands between them and joins their hands at the appropriate point in the service. In this photograph Sylvia and Peter are pictured after their wedding, holding a cardboard guitar to symbolise their musical activities.*

wore a much simpler dress that was said to suggest a medieval Italian gown. The issue of *Vogue* for April 1923, which reported her wedding, also featured a design for a 'Victorian' style wedding dress. 'Medieval' designs were popular again in the early 1930s and the high-waisted 'Empire' line of the mid 1960s was only a modern version of Regency dress. This style was to remain popular for wedding dresses well into the 1970s. The Paris couturiers Cardin and Courreges both showed 'space age' clothes in their 1966 and 1968 collections – many of these were similar to Mary Quant's basic designs but were carried a step further in various synthetic and hitherto unthought-of materials – but only a few girls wore 'space' inspired wedding dresses, although several did wear Mary Quant type mini-dresses and coats in which to be married. Most girls preferred to look back in time, and, besides the 'Regency' look, the late Victorian and Edwardian periods were probably the most popular for brides and bridesmaids.

For men at weddings in the 1950s and 1960s there was little deviation from the accepted convention of morning dress, usually

90. *By the second half of the 1960s the mini-dress, way above the knee, was high fashion. This 1968 bride, whose wedding outfit is now in Carlisle Museum, wore a mini-dress and matching coat in an ivory man-made fibre which resembles linen with a woollen finish. The dress was sleeveless and plain with a round neckline and a seam down the centre front, having a line of machine top stitching on either side. The coat had long sleeves and a high neckline with a pointed collar. It fastened with three self-covered buttons and had three more to give the appearance of a double-breasted fastening. The bride wore a spray of flowers on the top of her head with a ribbon streamer over each shoulder.*

91. *A formal wedding in 1969, when John Love married Susan Kirk. Black top hats had by this time gone out of fashion, and grey was the accepted colour. The bride's dress was reminiscent of the styles of the 1890s (see picture 29), but she wore a single large flower on top of her head to hold her voluminous veil (see picture 86).*

hired, or dark lounge suit. The latter came to be regarded over the two decades as a formal way of dressing. While morning dress changed very little – grey gradually taking the place of black for hats, jackets and trousers – the lounge suit, originally the casual wear of the well-to-do Victorians, changed constantly, although slightly. Some of these changes were influenced by 'cult' fashions among very young men of pre-marriageable age, or by fashions from overseas, notably America. Thus the padded shoulders and long jackets of the early 1950s 'teddy boys' heralded a fashion for longer lapels on adult suits. Similarly American styled 'draped' (cut looser across the chest) jackets became popular as men realised that they were more comfortable than the skimpier British cut. When the heavy padding of the mid 1950s became lighter in the 1960s the long lapels which had balanced it became shorter again, but the looser fitting jackets remained in fashion.

Turn-ups are another example. Originally introduced on lounge suits at the end of the nineteenth century, they were alternately fashionable and unfashionable until 1941, when they were abolished to save material. However, 'demob' suits were cut with turn-ups, which were then fashionable throughout the 1950s.

92. *The high-waisted Empire line was the most popular style for wedding dresses and bridesmaids' dresses for just over ten years. It was introduced in the mid 1960s and there was still a variation of the design in the pattern books of 1980. In this photograph, comptometer operator Joan Dando wore a white satin Empire line dress trimmed with white lace daisies for her marriage to merchant seaman Terence Micklewright, who wore a lounge suit. Their wedding was at Whitethorn Avenue Methodist church, Banstead, Surrey, in June 1970, and the picture was taken inside the church, an action which would have been unthinkable before the 1960s.*

By the mid 1960s turn-ups had gone out of fashion. Ties, too, have varied in width since the Second World War, from very wide in 1950 to very narrow, then wider again. Bow ties have always been a less fashionable alternative but were not often worn at weddings. Ties of all sorts were abandoned altogether for casual wear in the late 1960s but remained a mark of formality and were therefore always worn at weddings. Colours for wedding suits and ties were always a conservative grey or dark blue. Not until the 1970s did formal fashions for men attempt to become more colourful and lively and some young men at weddings began to rival, or even outshine, the bride.

Tradition and change, 1970-9
In the 1970s there were drastic changes in fashion and the following of fashion, as in other things. Some people clung to the past and their wedding photographs could have been taken in Edwardian times, or at any time between 1930 and 1980; others

were definitely of the 1970s simply because what they wore to their weddings would have been unthinkable, or at least unobtainable, previously. Added to this mixture of conservatism and adventure in the British people were the wedding customs of a growing number of immigrants from all parts of the world and of various religious faiths, so that wedding photographers during the 1970s recorded a wider variety of wedding fashions than at any other time. The clothes may change, but custom, which is the greater part of tradition, dies hard. There are still parts of the British Isles where weddings are honoured by practices that have been observed for generations past. People still dance all night at Scottish weddings; in Somerset the wedding party is locked in the churchyard and only released on payment of a handful of loose coins; and in Guernsey the newly married couple place a coin on the head of a prehistoric stone figure in the churchyard.

However, each time a tradition is honoured it is changed a

93. *In a mixture of English and Tibetan ceremony Tswewang Norbu Pemba and his bride, Lhakpa Dolma, were married at Hertford Registry Office in August 1971. Both wore Tibetan ceremonial clothes, the bridegroom resplendent in a long orange robe patterned with circular emblems in gold, and the bride in a dark blue long sleeveless robe worn over a white silk blouse. Her costume was completed by an apron made up of three strips of fabric constructed out of short lengths of multicoloured silk ribbon. At the reception, held in a very English garden, the bride and some of her Tibetan women friends performed a traditional Tibetan dance for the guests, who each presented the bride and groom with white silk scarves as well as wedding presents. These scarves are a Tibetan tradition, each one symbolising good luck. Their wedding cake was a conventional English iced fruit cake and the reception lasted only four hours instead of the traditional Buddhist three days and three nights. Photograph by the 'Hertfordshire Mercury'.*

94. *Wearing a hair-style typical of the early 1970s but a traditionally styled grey dress-suit and top hat, best man Steve Wells adjusts the white carnation worn by his friend Alistair Emblem at his wedding on 5th May 1973.*

95. *After the wedding Alistair poses with his bride, Jenny, on the steps of the church. Jenny wore a boat-necked, high-waisted dress of white brocade with wide flowing sleeves and a gauzy veil of very fine nylon. Her bridesmaids wore high-waisted dresses made in a flowered pink fabric in a style reminiscent of Jane Austen's heroines. Their head-dresses were simple white Juliet caps and they carried posies of spring flowers.*

96. *There are no bridesmaids or best man at a Quaker wedding, nor is there an officiating minister or priest (for all Friends are equal in the sight of God). On an appointed day the bridal pair sit side by side and at an appropriate point in the meeting they stand and each says to the assembly: 'Friends, I (name) take this, my friend (name), to be my wife/husband, promising with God's help to be unto her/him a faithful and loving husband/wife so long as we both on Earth shall live.' After the service every member of the meeting signs the register as a witness. There are few outward trappings of the 'traditional' wedding, and a 'best' ordinarily fashionable dress is worn by the bride and his normal 'meeting' suit by the bridegroom. At this wedding, at the Friends' Meeting House, Hertford, in 1974, Pamela Dunning married Hansueli Dietiker, a Swiss Quaker. She wore a full-length Empire line dress with scoop neck and long sleeves in a pale yellow voile striped with orange satin and carried a posy of flowers. He wore a lounge suit with a black bow tie and white carnation. The photograph was taken by Mr R. Young of Studio Young, Hoddesdon.*

little. This is as true of the British white wedding, which may well be the style chosen by a couple who were born, or whose parents were born, in the West Indies, central Africa or the Far East, as it is of the Hindu or Moslem wedding solemnised in a ceremony imported from overseas by English-speaking young people born in Britain of immigrant parents or grandparents. The photographs in this section of the book cover a wide spectrum of weddings, not only various Christian denominations, but also Hindu, Moslem, Buddhist and Jewish. All weddings are a pledging of two people to each other, a public declaration of the joining of their two lives at a celebration at which their friends and relatives wish them well. People choose their clothes for a wedding with deliberate care, but in the last quarter of the twentieth century the choice can be as wide as the world.

The average British bride and groom, however, have followed British fashion, even if only subconsciously. In the first part of the

97. *It is an old Guernsey custom for a bride and bridegroom to leave an offering of flowers or coins on the head of the prehistoric statue or menhir by the gate of St Martin's church in St Peter Port. The statue is known locally as La Gran'mere du Chimquiere (the Grandmother of the Cemetery). This photograph was taken in August 1975 and shows a Guernsey bride and groom placing a coin on the head of 'Gran'mere' as they leave the churchyard after the wedding. The bride wore an Empire line dress with lace sleeves and her veil was fastened to the back of a plain Juliet cap. The bridegroom wore a lounge suit and a red flower in his buttonhole. In the 1960s and 1970s coloured flowers began to replace the white carnations that had been worn by bridegrooms for most of the twentieth century.*

decade colour was important, not just for the bride, whose 'white' wedding dress could vary from pale cream to deep coffee (sometimes even shading from one to the other in the same dress), but more particularly for the bridegroom and his friends, young men with shoulder-length hair, who wore jackets of dark green or maroon over wide flared trousers. In their wedding photographs the generations stand out sharply, father and son almost appearing to come from two different worlds. Their brides wore large floppy hats rather than veils and when not in a 'white' dress wore small flower-print cottons with long skirts, often trimmed with lace or ric-rac braid. But this trend did not last. By the mid 1970s young bridegrooms, even with shoulder-length hair, were wearing conventional lounge suits or morning suits again and brides were wearing veils. The floppy hats and flower-print country-style dresses remained popular for bridesmaids, adult or children, for the whole of the decade.

98 (right). *A modern Jewish wedding. All Jewish weddings must take place under a canopy. This is a remembrance of the ancient two-stage Jewish wedding, a binding 'betrothal' ceremony, followed at a later date by the actual wedding and the consummation of the marriage in the Chuppah (the Hebrew word for bridal chamber). Since the sixteenth century the betrothal and the wedding have usually been combined in one ceremony under the canopy, called the Chuppah, to symbolise the bridal chamber. Under Jewish law, weddings do not have to be in a synagogue, but today most of them are held there. The wedding in this photograph was held at Kingston upon Thames Liberal Synagogue in July 1977 and was between Diana Barton of Epsom and Benny Cantor of Sweden. It is traditional for men to cover their heads in the synagogue and the bridegroom wore a white 'festival' skullcap, known in Hebrew as a 'kappel' (see also picture 40). The bride wore a white organdie dress with a*

waist-length transparent shoulder cape. Jewish wedding dresses are normally in the fashion of their own time and this bride chose to wear a hat because large hats for brides (of any religion) were fashionable in the mid 1970s. Photograph by Roy Cook of Hampton Hill, Middlesex.

99 (left). *For bridesmaids, adult and tiny, variations on the Empire line were the most popular style of the 1970s. Flower-sprigged Laura Ashley type cottons were the most popular fabrics. This photograph shows Elizabeth and Vicky, sister and niece of Angela Carey, who were bridesmaids at her wedding at Weybridge in October 1977.*

100. *In 1978 Mrs Anthea James married for the second time. In contrast to her first wedding
(see picture 87) this was an informal ceremony. Her bridesmaids were her daughter and her
niece (the child of the bridesmaid at her first wedding), and the bride and bridesmaids wore
home-made layered dresses and embroidered white petticoats, Anthea in a cream voile
smock over a cream crepe silk-flounced skirt, and Lily, her little niece, in a pale pink viyella
dress and a white lawn frilled pinafore. Long dresses, like the deep-red wool pinafore dress
with its white petticoat worn by the bride's teenage daughter, Emily, were worn every day by
many young women in the mid and late 1970s, making the 'old-fashioned country girl' style
part of the modern town scene. The wedding was on Easter Monday and the flowers, picked
from the garden, included cream jonquils, pink bergenias and pale green hellebores.
Emily's posy had flame-coloured early tulips as well, to match the red of her dress. The
wedding party arrived at and left the church in two Land Rovers, the normal mode of
transport of the bridegroom, Adrian Jarvis, and his brother-in-law, Matthew Hyde, who
afterwards took this photograph. Both men wore typical 1970s lounge suits with wide-legged
trousers.*

101. *Many weddings at registry offices in the 1970s were examples of 'fancy dress' rather than traditional wedding dress or best 'ordinary' dress. The fancy dress ranged from blue jeans and embroidered Afghan coats (worn by a pop star and his bride) to 'space age' clothes inspired by the Paris designers Cardin and Courreges. When science fiction bookseller Richard Van der Voort married Marion Dougall at Richmond, Surrey, registry office in June 1978 he wore tan-coloured corduroy trousers tucked into cowboy boots with a vivid green shirt embroidered by his bride with an orange and white dragon across the back. His bride wore an iridescent dark blue-green caftan and carried a matching handbag and a silver horseshoe decorated with white flowers and ribbons.*

For brides who did not want a white wedding the choice was wide. The 1970s saw the slow demise of the mini-skirt, and during this time the full-length maxi-skirt was an acceptable alternative fashion, so that at many mid 1970s weddings the bride and her contemporary women guests wore floor-length dresses in a variety of colours and fabrics, hand-printed Indian cottons or muslins probably being predominant. In an affluent society newness is not necessarily considered a virtue; the younger generation's rejection of the values of their parents showed in the patchwork fabrics, the boiler suits and the 'used' or faded denim jeans that they chose to wear every day. The repercussions were wide and, almost as a subconscious revolt against the crisp,

general acceptance that clothes should both express the personality of the wearer and be appropriate for the occasion. White was firmly considered the conventional colour for a wedding dress, and since in 1980 white or ivory were fashionable colours for general wear there was a wide range of clothes available in these colours.

Brides, therefore, could choose anything from a long, romantic trained dress in a Victorian or Edwardian inspired style (the 'Empire' line seemed finally to be disappearing) to a sophisticated suit of just above mid-calf length in any fabric from silk or lace to pure wool, or a day or evening trouser suit style. Many grooms still wore morning dress, although many more wore lounge suits since for an increasing number of young men the lounge suit had become formal wear only. Bridesmaids were no longer considered essential except to a full church service where the bride wore a long dress and train. Even then only one or two bridesmaids accompanied the bride. Their clothes matched the bride's dress in style but were coloured where hers was white. A bride in a short dress or a trouser suit did not have any bridesmaids.

No one can tell what the future may hold for fashion, whether for weddings or for everyday clothes. The freedom of choice of 1980 may give way to more rigid rules in dress. But one tradition will remain, that a wedding is a celebration; the clothes will change but a bride will be a bride and a groom a groom, now and always, following the fashions of their own time and place. In all ages, may the world wish them well.

---

104 (opposite). *A Hindu wedding is the linking of two families rather than the union of two individuals and all the members of these two families have a part to play in the ceremony. The bride is hidden at the start of the wedding and it is the bridegroom who arrives in his best clothes carrying flowers and wearing a garland given to him by his parents. In the upper photograph, Lalit Pandya, spiritual head of the Kingston and Surbiton Hindu community, watches carefully as the bridegroom, wearing a lightweight fawn western-style lounge suit and brown tie, is greeted by the mother of the bride. Surrounded by members of both families, she shows him the five symbols of household goods wrapped in a scarf and asks him if he is ready to undertake the responsibilities of marriage. During the ceremony the bride and groom remove their shoes and their feet are washed. The groom removes his original garland and gives it to his best man, then exchanges fresh garlands with the bride. Their right hands are clasped and covered with a white scarf and a rope is placed round their necks to link them together. They then walk four times round a fire that represents life, the groom taking the lead three times, the bride for the fourth time, to symbolise that they will care for each other through the four stages of life (lower photograph). This wedding was celebrated under a decorated canopy in the ballroom of the Queen's Hotel, Crystal Palace, in the summer of 1980. The bride wore a pink and silver sari. She and her groom exchanged red and white garlands.*

105 (above). *At the wedding of Sue Handscomb, of the Weybridge Ladies Rowing Club, and Ian McNuff, of the 1980 British Olympic rowing team, the bride's clubmates and the groom's team-mates formed a guard of honour, holding rowing blades under which the newly-weds walked to carry out a good-luck ritual, imported by the national squad's coach, a Czechoslovak. As the bride and groom left St James's church, Weybridge, a blade was lowered, blocking their path, and the groom lifted his bride over it, then sawed it in half to regain her side, to the cheers of their companions. Sue wore a voile dress with lace-edged long sleeves over a plain silk slip. Like several brides of 1980, she wore no veil but pinned flowers in her hair to match her bouquet. Ian wore his Olympic blazer and tie, as did his attendant team-mates. Photographs by John Shore of Weybridge.*

106 (opposite). *Robin Hill, an aircraft design engineer, proudly presents his student bride, Penny, after their marriage at Kingston upon Thames registry office in July 1980. He wore a brown striped lounge suit and Penny wore an ivory crepe silk cape-tunic over a fitted sleeveless one-piece trouser suit. She wore a single flower in her hair and carried a delicate bouquet of carnations, chrysanthemums and fern.*

8. Places to visit

Most museums that collect costumes have wedding dresses in their storerooms. Costume displays are constantly changed, however, since the clothes deteriorate when on show. Large collections of wedding dresses are held in the following museums and if not on public display can be seen by appointment.

Bethnal Green Museum of Childhood, Cambridge Heath Road, London E2 9PA. Telephone: 01-980 2415.

Bexhill Manor Costume Museum, Manor House Gardens, Bexhill Old Town, Bexhill, East Sussex TN20 2AP. Telephone: Bexhill-on-Sea (0424) 215361.

Castle Howard Costume Galleries, Castle Howard, York YO6 7DA. Telephone: Coneysthorpe (065 384) 333 extension 34.

Croxteth Hall, Croxteth Hall Lane, Liverpool. Telephone: Merseyside County Museums, 051-207 0001 or 5451.

Gallery of English Costume, Platt Fields, Rusholme, Manchester M14 5LL. Telephone: 061-224 5217.

The Hollytrees, High Street, Colchester, Essex CO1 1UG. Telephone: Colchester (0206) 712493.

Museum of Costume, Alfred Street, Bath, Avon BA1 2QH. Telephone: Bath (0225) 61111.

Museum of Costume, Camphill House, Queens Park, Pollokshaws Road, Glasgow G41 2EW. Telephone: 041-632 1350.

Museum of Costume and Textiles, 51 Castle Gate, Nottingham NG1 6AF. Telephone: Nottingham (0602) 411881.

Museum of London, London Wall, London EC2Y 5HN. Telephone: 01-600 3699.

Royal Albert Memorial Museum, Queen Street, Exeter, Devon EX4 3RX. Telephone: Exeter (0392) 56724.

Royal Museums of Scotland, Chambers Street, Edinburgh EH1 1JF. Telephone: 031-225 7534.

Royal Museums of Scotland, Queen Street, Edinburgh EH2 1JD. Telephone: 031-557 3550.

Tullie House Museum and Art Gallery, Castle Street, Carlisle, Cumbria CA3 8TP. Telephone: Carlisle (0228) 34781.

Victoria and Albert Museum, Cromwell Road, South Kensington, London SW7 2RL. Telephone: 01-589 6371.

Wygston's House Museum of Costume, 12 Applegate, Leicester. Telephone: Leicester (0533) 554100 extension 213.

York Castle Museum, Tower Street, York YO1 1RY. Telephone: York (0904) 53611.

9. Further reading

Anthony, Ilid. *Costumes of the Welsh People*. National Museum of Wales, Welsh Folk Museum.
Argy, Josie, and Riches, Wendy. *Britain's Royal Brides*. Sphere Books, 1977.
Baker, Margaret. *Wedding Customs and Folklore*. David and Charles, 1977.
Cunnington, Phyllis, and Lucas, Catherine. *Costume for Births, Marriages and Deaths*. A. and C. Black, 1972.
Gallery of English Costume. *Weddings*. City of Manchester, 1976/7.
Mansfield, Alan, and Cunnington, Phyllis. *English Costume in the Twentieth Century*. Faber and Faber, 1973.
Monserrat, Ann. *And the Bride Wore . . .* Gentry Books, 1973.
Royal Weddings in 'Vogue'. Conde Nast Publications, 1981.
Stevenson, Pauline. *Bridal Fashions*. Ian Allan, 1978.
Warwick, Christopher. *The Royal Brides*. Leslie Frewin, 1975.
Warwick, Christopher. *Two Centuries of Royal Weddings*. Arthur Barker Ltd, 1980.
Willet, C., and Cunnington, Phyllis. *English Costume in the Nineteenth Century*. Faber and Faber, 1959.

Acknowledgements

A book like this cannot be written without the help of a great many people and the author records her grateful thanks to her colleagues, friends, family and members of the public who loaned photographs and patiently answered her questions. In particular she would like to thank her husband, Mr Howard Lansdell (Honorary Secretary of the Historical Group of the Royal Photographic Society), both for copying many of the photographs and making available his own researches into the history of photography, Mrs Marion Van der Voort for typing the text (and for the loan of the Dougall scrapbooks) and Mrs Anthea Jarvis of the Merseyside Museums Service, without whose help and encouragement the book would have been very much the poorer. She would also like to acknowledge the help received from Ms Kate Rankine of Carlisle Museum and Art Gallery, Miss Jane Tozer of the Gallery of English Costume at Manchester, Miss Jane Carmichael of the Imperial War Museum, Mrs Joan Kendal of the Costume Society and Mrs Pam Fletcher-Jones of the Kingston Group for Racial Understanding.

Photographs and other illustrations are acknowledged as follows: by gracious permission of Her Majesty the Queen, 10, 11, 14 and 50; Mr G. Allam, 33; Miss B. Anderson, 51; Associated Newspapers Ltd, 103; the Auld Kirk Museum, Glasgow, 54; Mr A. G. J. Ball, 53 (both pictures); Barcaldine Castle Museum and the National Museum of Antiquities of Scotland, 19; Mr and Mrs R. Barton, 98; Mr and Mrs F. Carey, 91, 94, 95 and 99; Carlisle Museum and Art Gallery, 4, 46, 64 and 90; Mr E. Chambre-Hardman, 85; City of Manchester Museums and Art Galleries, 24 and 67; Mrs E. Cladish, 60; Mrs B. Cooke 27 and 42; Mrs E. Creed, 86; Mr and Mrs P. Daniell, 65 and 102; Dundee Central Museum, 22; Mr and Mrs D. Ellis, 2 and 3; Fenton Photography Museum, 13 and 29; Mrs P. Fletcher-Jones, 40; Mrs E. Forde, 77; Mrs D. Geach, 47; Mr and Mrs A. Gibb, 83; Mrs H. Graham, 8 and 9; Guernsey Museum and Art Gallery, 97; Mrs D. Hanning, 6; Mr and Mrs B. Harrison, 56 and 62; Mr and Mrs E. Hazell, 49; Mr and Mrs W. Hill, 5, 36, 63 and 106; Imperial War Museum, 7, 68 and 69; Mr and Mrs A. Jarvis, 87 and 100; Kingston upon Thames Museum and Heritage Centre, 1; Mr and Mrs J. Kitson, 73; Lansdell Collection, 15, 21, 34, 38, 45, 52, 57, 61, 72, 78 and 88; Lieutenant Colonel and Mrs R. May, 82; Mr and Mrs I. McNuff, 105; Merseyside County Museums, 20 and 28 (both pictures); Merseyside County Museums and Mrs G. Povall, 55; Merseyside County Museums and Mrs N. Whilton, 74; Mr and Mrs T. Micklewright, 92; Mr Monty Moss of Moss Bros Ltd, 71; Mr and Mrs Motley, 70; Mr A. Newton, 43; Northumberland Record Office, 23; Mr Lalut Pandya, 104 (both pictures); Mr and Mrs T. D. Pemba, 93; Mrs B. Ranger, page 3; the Reeves Collection, by courtesy of the *Sunday Times* and Sussex Archaeological Society, 17 and 18; Mrs M. Reynolds, 12, 58; Mrs F. Rogers, 59; Mr and Mrs E. Rooke, 75; Science Museum, page 4; Mr and Mrs L. Stenning, 81; Mrs M. H. Taylor, 37 (both pictures) and front cover; Mr and Mrs R. Van der Voort, 25, 26 (both pictures), 30, 31, 39, 66 and 101; Mrs A. K. Vinicombe, 48; the *War Cry,* 89; Mrs R. Webb, 32; Weybridge Museum, 44, pages 1 and 2; Mr and Mrs R. White, 84; Mr and Mrs K. Wickham, 79 and 80; the Reverend and Mrs G. Wilkie, 76; Miss P. Williams, 16, 35 and 41; Mr R. Young, 96.

Index

Page numbers in italic refer to illustrations or their captions.